THE SHADOW AND THE PROBLEM OF EVIL

Five Examinations

Murray Stein (ed.)

CHIRON PUBLICATIONS • ASHEVILLE, NORTH CAROLINA

www.ChironPublications.com

Interior and cover design by Danijela Mijailovic
Front cover painting by Diane Stanley
Printed primarily in the United States of America.

ISBN 978-1-68503-193-0 paperback
ISBN 978-1-68503-194-7 hardcover
ISBN 978-1-68503-195-4 electronic
ISBN 978-1-68503-196-1 limited edition paperback

Library of Congress Cataloging-in-Publication Data

Names: Stein, Murray, 1943- editor.
Title: The shadow and the problem of evil : five examinations / Murray Stein (ed.).
Description: Asheville, North Carolina : Chiron Publications, [2023] | Includes bibliographical references. | Summary: "The Shadow And The Problem Of Evil: Five Examinations is a captivating and thought-provoking journey into the hidden recesses of the human psyche. Through a Jungian perspective, it offers insights into the nature of evil, the symbols that represent our shadows, and the profound impact of these hidden aspects on society and our ethical choices. It's a must-read for those seeking a deeper understanding of the human condition and the challenges we face in the modern world. Murray Stein's opening chapter, "The Shadow and the Problem of Evil," explores the fundamental question of the shadow's connection to evil and Mary Tomlinson introduces the intricate ways the shadow manifests symbolically in our psyche in "Symbols of Shadow and Evil." "The Atom Bomb and the Collective Confrontation with Evil,"examines how collective experiences, like the atomic bomb, force society to confront the shadow on a grand scale. "Paranoia: The Madness That Makes History" uncovers how paranoia shapes historical events. In "The Shadow and the Search for a New Ethic" Henry Abramovitch and Stein ponder the ethical implications of recognizing and integrating the shadow into our lives. Brigitte Egger's final chapter, "Human Shadow Revealed by the Ecological Crisis," explores how the ecological crisis serves as a mirror, reflecting our collective shadow and calling for a profound reevaluation of our relationship with the environment"-- Provided by publisher.
Identifiers: LCCN 2023052200 (print) | LCCN 2023052201 (ebook) | ISBN 9781685031930 (paperback) | ISBN 9781685031947 (hardcover) | ISBN 9781685031954 (ebook)
Subjects: LCSH: Shadow (Psychoanalysis) | Good and evil. | Jungian psychology.
Classification: LCC BF175.5.S55 S47 2024 (print) | LCC BF175.5.S55 (ebook) | DDC 150.19/54--dc23/eng/20231207
LC record available at https://lccn.loc.gov/2023052200
LC ebook record available at https://lccn.loc.gov/2023052201

Preface

Our time like no other in recent memory calls for serious reflection on the shadow and the problem of evil. The shadow is to be found within us all, of course, as we well know from our own psychoanalytic experiences and introspective self-examinations. But also and most dangerously it is found exceptionally on the loose among all the collectives of the world today. No people or nation seems free of it, and egregious acting out of blatant shadow projections and enactments are revealed in the media every day. Not that the media are without shadow enactments of their own. Mistrust of them runs deep. Where is truth to be found? This is a cry often heard among the people, and the answer to that question is ever more elusive.

Lest we be too overwhelmed with the realization of shadows everywhere in our own time, we should recall that previous ages have felt the same about theirs. One need only think of C.G. Jung facing two World Wars in Europe in his lifetime, both of them based on shadow projection and possession on the part of political leaders and the convinced masses. No age is free of evil; it is ever stalking through back alleys, homes, and public forums. Perhaps today we have something of an advantage over ages past in the acquired awareness of shadow psychodynamics – projection, possession, enactment – which we have as a heritage of our psychoanalytic forebears. Freud was a master of shadow exposure of the hypocrisy rampant behind the carefully crafted and presented personas in his fin-de-siecle European culture, and Jung deepened our apprehension of the persistence and subtle intrusions of shadow dynamics in the "civilized" peoples of our time. Every age must face evil and discover the shadow at work in its own time and space. Mephistopheles is always on the prowl and adapts subtly to every age and clime.

The essays in this volume are intended to sharpen our eyes for shadow in our private and public lives. They were originally presented in the form of online lectures given through the Asheville Jung Society in 2016 and have been revised by the authors for this publication. The order in which they appear in this collection is the same as that in the lecture series.

Murray Stein, Goldiwil

Table of Contents

Introduction
The Shadow and the Problem of Evil

Murray Stein

Projection of Evil

Evil is something that is occupying collective consciousness tremendously throughout our world today because of all the violence that we see in the news, the acts of terrorism, wars of various kinds and sizes, and criminality. We see that violence and terror dominate the news almost to the exclusion of everything else. It's very unusual to see stories that are positive and upbeat. In other words, it's rare to see evidence of good in the world. Is this an extraordinary eruption of the shadow and evil in the world? Or is it an undercurrent that has always been there but is now popping up more blatantly, erupting in Paris, London, New York, the Middle East, in our homes, in our own neighborhoods, in our schools? Is this an eruption of the shadow of collective consciousness, both in projection and in reality?

Psychologically speaking, we need to distinguish between the projection of evil on the one hand—figures, symbols, events—and the reality of evil in the world. How do we separate them? How can we diminish the effects of projection that might interfere with our grasp of reality?

We know that what is unconscious appears to us in projections. To the extent that we are unconscious of evil in our own world or in ourselves, we are going to project it out into something or into somebody else. When this gets going strongly, we have the familiar psychopathology called paranoia, which is the projection of evil into the world around. Paranoia takes over a personality when a vague sense of danger threatens from the unknown and the unfamiliar. That's where we project the unconscious contents, into the unknown and the unfamiliar. Often world leaders can get caught up in paranoid projections and act on them. This can change the course of history, as we know.

The simple fact of otherness in a person or in a population can strike fear into the minds of individuals and collectives and invites spontaneous projections. When you don't know who or what they are, and there is some notion of threat in the air as we experience it today with a vast migration of foreign populations into our home spaces, the otherness on our streets, on our television screens, and in our minds, it invites projections because you don't know who they are. You have a vague sense of threat, a suspicion that they want what we have, and so you project some of the worst of our own shadow fantasies into their otherness. There are, of course, enactments of violence in response. The carrier of the projection will sometimes be activated to carry out what is projected. There is thus a malicious cycle of projection and enactment of violence, which we call evil, in our midst. This repetitious cycle of projection and enactment starts accumulating, and we have a very difficult time finding a way to stop it or break into it.

On the Meaning of the Term "Evil"

The term "evil" is being used in the public domain today in a way I don't recall from my youth. Today, however, we hear it frequently in the media and in conversation. This is likely a product of the extreme divisions among parties and nations in our present world. The opposites good-and-evil have become constellated in the public mind. And it's hard to sort out who are the "good guys" and who are the "bad guys" because each side makes out the other to be evil and their side to be totally on the side of the good. We are forced, therefore, to reflect on what evil actually is simply by virtue of living in our times.

The rhetoric of evil in politics was given a strong push in 1983 by then-U.S. President Ronald Reagan in a speech that became known as the Evil Empire Speech. This was delivered to a group of fundamentalist Christians in Florida. In it, President Reagan referred to the Soviet Union as the Evil Empire. This phrase was picked up in the media, of course, and used a great deal to indicate President Reagan's negative moral evaluation of communism and what the Soviet Union stood for at that time. He identified the Soviet Union, in effect, with satanic forces active in the political world. Naturally, the Soviets hurled the same epithet at the West.

Understandably, it is very upsetting to be labeled evil. Nobody wants to be identified as evil. Everybody wants to be good and to see the other guy as the purveyor of evil. President Reagan was famous for splitting the world into good and evil. This terminology is moralistic and reflects his personal psychology, but it also resonates with many. It sounds like science fiction to speak of an Evil Empire. This gives the phrase an archetypal quality. The rhetoric of evil in politics continued when President George W. Bush in a speech in 2002 given shortly after 9/11 and the attack on New York City used the phrase "axis of evil" to speak of three countries aligned against America. Iran, Iraq, and North Korea were pegged as evil for promoting terrorism and for presumably seeking to acquire weapons of mass destruction to further their designs against the West. President Bush, like Reagan, chose a moralistic, quasitheological division of the world into those who favor good (our side) and those who favor evil (the other side). The choice of language was readily reciprocated.

Speaking in the terms of good and evil in public life, however, is a usage that is unfamiliar to modernity, in which one tries to be morally neutral and scientific. What is evil, after all? Can it be defined and measured quantitively? Some psychologists have tried to study it empirically, and professional specialties like Forensic Psychiatry have working definitions and treatment procedures.[1] In scientific papers, however, the term "evil" is rarely employed. The very word touches on something basically irrational and symbolic with strong mythic and religious overtones.

Jung himself and those following him, however, have frequently taken up the subject of "the problem of evil," perhaps precisely because it has symbolic and mythic references. We see this theme vividly confronted in *The Red Book: Liber Novus*, wherein Jung was dealing with it in his active imaginations and fantasies during his midlife crisis. In his published writings after that, he refers frequently to the problem of evil and relates it to the psychological concept of

---

[1] See for example J. Reid Meloy, *The Psychopathic Mind*.

the shadow as an aspect of the human personality. Discussion of the human personality therefore necessarily includes the problem of evil.

A series of lectures given at the C.G. Jung Institute in Zurich in 1959-60 by various members of the faculty and possibly attended by Jung himself bears the title *Das Böse*, and these were published in 1961 with the same title. It appeared in English translation six years later with the simple title *Evil*. The eight authors approach the subject of evil from a number of different disciplines: mythology (Karl Kerényi), Eastern religions (Geo Widengren), Christianity (Victor Maag), Fairy Tales (Marie-Louise von Franz), cinema (Martin Schlappner), psychology (Liliane Frey-Rohn), philosophy (Karl Löwith), and creativity (Karl Schmid). In the Introduction to the volume of essays, the Curatorium writes:

> From time immemorial the best minds have pondered the questions: What is the source of evil? Why does it exist? What is its true nature? They have arrived at the most divergent conclusions. Yet all attempts to define it and to find ways of overcoming it have been unsuccessful.[2]

No one has been able to offer a generally acceptable answer.

In the essay titled "Evil from a Psychological Point of View," Liliane Frey-Rohn, who was a member of the Institute's Curatorium at the time, wrote: "Evil is a phenomenon that exists and has always existed only in the human world."[3] She

---

[2] *Evil,* p. xiii.
[3] Ibid., p. 153.

limits her discussion of evil to humanity and does not consider evil as a natural phenomenon, which is sometimes done in theology and philosophy where evil can be treated as a broader category. Even though animals might be vicious and at times violent, she excludes the animal kingdom from the discussion of evil and limits it to the human world. She notes that there is no form of religion, ethics, or community life in which evil is not an important topic. Ethics, which is a cognitive discipline dedicated to sorting out good and evil at all levels, attempts to bring rigor to what are otherwise intuitive distinctions and are subject to distortion based on complex bias and projection. Every human group on earth that has ever lived and that we know of and can study has some sense of good and evil, but not all speak about it with the same level of intellectual discrimination. Nevertheless, all have conventions that teach what is good and bad, which include instruction on how to behave toward others, toward oneself, toward the natural world, and how to live together in community.

It is difficult, however, as Frey-Rohn confesses, to give a precise definition of what we mean, psychologically, by the terms good and evil. We might have to be content to say there is the *problem* of evil, as something to think about but not foreclose with a strict definition. This leaves room for debate and further reflection. Something may appear to be evil at one point in history or in a specific context but look quite different at a later time or in another context.

One thing to keep in mind in reflecting on the problem of evil is that good and evil are a pair of opposites. It's impossible to know the one without knowledge of the other. This discriminating ability is what Adam and Eve got when they ate the fruit of the tree of the knowledge of good and evil. It's a type of knowledge that human beings have by virtue of the fall from innocence and the experience of shame. Knowledge of evil must include knowledge of the good. If people are shameless and experience no guilt or remorse for committing violent acts against others, they can be judged guilty by others and by the law, but in their own eyes, they are innocent because they do not know the difference between good and evil. Young children and psychopaths share this condition. Children are not held accountable by the law, but adult psychopaths are because they should know the difference. But perhaps they do not, in which case one speaks of the criminally insane and holds them accountable in a different way.

Levels of Consciousness

Before proceeding further with this discussion of consciousness of the difference between good and evil, it might be useful to reflect a bit on several levels of consciousness. Knowledge is a result of conscious operations, cognitive and emotional. It is important, therefore, that we take into account the type or level of consciousness that is producing this knowledge. There is a stage of preknowledge, and there are several stages of advanced knowledge based on levels of consciousness.

In his paper "The Spirit Mercurius," Jung describes five different levels of consciousness.[4] The first level is what he called *participation mystique*, a term he adopted from the philosopher and anthropologist, Lucien Lévi-Bruhl (1857-1939) and used for his own purposes in psychology. This is a type of consciousness in which there is no distinction

---

[4] C.G. Jung, "The Spirit Mercurius," CW 13, paras. 247-249.

between archetype and object. It's a consciousness in which psyche and objects are totally identified with one another. Psychologically, an aspect of the archetypal self is identified with the object, and this gives the object magical powers. It is when human psyches are so closely identified with objects that the objects so identified with obtain a controlling power over the psyches so invested. This state of consciousness is associated with early childhood. The infant doesn't have a sense of self as separate from mother's body or the object world around. The infant feels at one with these objects. In anthropology and ethnology, this level of consciousness is related to animism, where objects have mystical powers because mana permeates them. Among various aboriginal groups in Central Australia, the churinga stone is powerful and can magically affect other objects or people because it contains a spirit, perhaps of an ancestor. It is a "power object." With respect to our discussion, evil at this level of consciousness is in a state of identity with the object to which it is attached. "That person is an evil witch," would be a typical expression of this level of consciousness. President Reagan's phrase "Evil Empire," referring to the Soviet Union, signifies this level of consciousness. The archetype and the object are one.

The second stage of consciousness makes a distinction between the object and the content projected on it. The lines are less blurred. These powers—gods, goddesses, spirits of various kinds—are distinct and transcendent. They are not identified with the object but live apart in a metaphysical realm. They might enter into an object occasionally. Temples are created for them. Sometimes they are there, and sometimes they are not. The ancient Israelite Ark of the Covenant was like this. Sometimes the Lord was present and sometimes not. He was not fixed to the place or the object. The object was separate. In classical Greek religion, the gods and goddesses would occasionally reside in a temple or in a statue, but they are not limited to the object. They exceed the object in their ontology; they have their own standing. If the object is destroyed, they are not destroyed. We would say projection is taking place, but this isn't *participation mystique* anymore. The object, a statue say, might just be a piece of wood at one moment, while during rituals it might invested with sacred presence. Sometimes projection is at work and sometimes it isn't. A degree of autonomy exists in the spirit world now and in the world of consciousness. Consciousness and the unconscious are more separate, not as entangled. Consciousness is more separate from the object world. It is still a type of mythological consciousness but more independent from the powers of the invisible world of the spirits. For purposes of our discussion, a person or nation may sometimes be possessed by evil but not always so. Germany under Hitler was possessed, but previously during Goethe's time and afterward during Konrad Adenauer's time it was not. Sometimes my neighbor is taken over by the spirit of evil, but at other times she is just herself, a normal human being with decent manners.

After that, Jung writes, there is a third stage of consciousness, and this is where a clear discrimination between good and evil enters. A higher type of ethical reflection is now possible. It can now be determined that there are good spirits and there are evil spirits. This type of consciousness was characteristic of the European Middle Ages, when nature and the countryside were inhabited by a variety of spirits, ghosts, demons, and goblins, some of them good and some evil, or they fall on a spectrum between good and evil. The evil spirits can possess you and do harmful things to you, make you sick, trip you up, create accidents. Other spirits are good and can help you, can heal your stomachache or your broken arm. In fairy tales, too, there are good and evil spirits. These spirits all exist outside of the human psyche, but they can enter and take possession of people, like complexes. They live in another realm, a spirit realm, and have their own metaphysical reality. This is still mythological consciousness but able to make distinctions between good and evil aspects of the totality of spirits.

The clear distinction between good and evil that now comes into play in this state consciousness brings with it a requirement of responsibility. If one knows the difference between good and evil spirits, one can take some responsibility for one's preferences of the one or the other. At this point, ethical reflection is possible for people. They can choose between good spirits and evil spirits, and they are therefore held accountable for their actions even if the power motivating them ultimately is external to their psyches. Human beings are in a position to make ethical judgments about various options of behavior and conduct. At this third level of consciousness, however, there is still a sense of evil as a power unto itself. It exists outside the human being in a metaphysical realm. In some religions, there is a very strong dualistic setup between a good God and an evil God who engaged in an eternal struggle for dominance. Evil wants destruction and chaos, and the Good God wants creation and order. Good and evil are active here on the mythological level. Human consciousness is aware of the struggle between them but is not able to intervene on behalf of the one or the other.

Then we come to the Enlightenment and modernity and to the fourth stage of consciousness. Now there is a complete denial of metaphysical reality, of spirits good, bad, or neutral. Is it God speaking to us with a still small voice? Is it an evil demon tempting us to give ourselves over to sin? It doesn't matter because they don't exist. They are nothing but figments of the imagination and have no meaning. Only material reality exists. If you can't measure it, it doesn't exist. If you can't smell, taste, touch it, it doesn't exist. That whole mythological world is banished as empty superstition, and all theological religions are considered to be based on an elaboration of fantasy. Nature and human history have been demythologized. Rational explanations based on scientific evidence will account for all behavior and will eventually eliminate all mystery. This is modernity, and this is where modern medicine and psychiatry have their home. The distinction between good and evil has to be made by rational argument based on agreed upon principles and not on referrals to good and evil spirits taking possession of the human mind and heart. Ethics becomes a highly rational operation, a product of cognitive reflection based on established and agreed upon principles and values. This has created a crisis because it is very difficult and maybe even impossible to find a rock-solid basis for the values that are to act as the foundation for discrimination between good and evil. One cannot any longer appeal to Divine Will or Commandments for authorization as in premodern times. Consciousness is on its own. Philosophy has succeeded religion. This places an enormous burden on ego-consciousness and the rational mind. Even the concepts of good and evil are called into question because they are reminiscent of an earlier age.

Modern thought tries to account for behavior not on the basis of good and evil spirits inhabiting us or doing things to us, but on the basis of our genetic makeup, our acculturation and conditioning, our childhood; or on the basis of our medical health, our neurological networks, or our inherent susceptibility to outer influences like the media. The terms good and evil now disappear from the discussion of ethics in the scientific literature. Such terminology is taboo. This is why it seems strange that it's coming back into popular usage again, which obviously does not conform to this scientific worldview. As soon as the discussion of good and evil reenters, we're into another interpretive territory.

Jung now takes us step further in his discussion of levels of consciousness and says in so many words: You can decide that the metaphysical reality of these spirits doesn't exist and they are just fantasy, but fantasy counts, fantasy has power. This brings us to the fifth level of consciousness.

When you delve deeply enough into the unconscious, you realize that these spirits, goblins, good and evil figures do exist there. Jung calls them archetypal images, and they do exist but not in the way it was thought they did in medieval times. They exist in our psyches. This is a major discovery. It's as though the telescope has been turned around and instead of looking out into the skies above and finding the gods and goddesses in the constellations, it is aimed into the inner world where one finds the same thing. "As above, so below," as the Emerald Tablet says. We realize that what mythologies did was inscribe the human psyche into the heavens, and now we're looking at these figures within the psyche itself. This is the reality of the psyche. The spirits have psychic reality. They live in the world of the unconscious.

The world of the unconscious is every bit as real and powerful as it was in its externalized form in premodern times and cultures. Modern people too can become possessed by these powers, which we call complexes, archetypal energies, psychic forces, and so on. We can be possessed by them to the extent that we lose consciousness of ourselves as distinct from them. We can be taken over by fantasies that we swear are real because we are unconscious of them and we're projecting them. We're actually experiencing them, and we create a narrative and an account of reality based on them. The subject of the existence of good and evil has shifted locations. We are talking about good and evil in the psychic world.

There is also a sixth stage of consciousness that Jung implies in his late writings. We can call this the awareness of *unus mundus* ("one world"), the awareness of synchronicity. This is the intuitive awareness that the inner figures called archetypes are not limited to the human psyche but correspond to patterns in extrapsychic reality. There is an ontological reality that both are grounded in. If that is true, what we call good and evil are constructive and destructive patterns of energy that our experience of good and evil recapitulate on a human emotional and mental level.

The Problem of Evil in Forensic Psychiatry and Psychology

A book published in 2010 titled, *Forensic Psychiatry: Influences of Evil,* introduces the topic of evil, which had been assiduously eliminated from the world of scientific and medical descriptions of human behavior, back into the discussion. The book includes a number of essays in which the subject of evil is brought into psychiatric reflection. The editor, Tom Mason, contributes an essay titled "An Archeology of the Psychopath: *The Medicalization of Evil.*" Mason argues that the psychopath has become a "clinical object" and evil has thereby been medicalized, but this does not explain it. The word "evil," which has moralistic associations attached to it, no longer appears in the literature about diagnosis and treatment of psychopathy. Some religious people claim the medicalization of evil threatens "to break down all the safeguards of our Christian civilization, by destroying , if possible, all grounds for human responsibility."[5] When evil becomes illness and gets medicalized, it loses its moral value. "Beginning with notions of good and evil, right and wrong, and freewill and determinism, the ground was set for the creation of the psychopath as a clinical entity."[6] Mason's article excavates the history of this move and brings the problematics into stark relief.

Stephen Diamond, who puts together a combination of Freudian, Jungian, and existentialist thought to create what he calls existential depth psychology, has worked for many years with violent offenders in California prisons. His essay in *Forensic Psychiatry* is titled "Violence as Secular Evil: Forensic Evaluation and Treatment of Violent Offenders from the Viewpoint of Existential Death Psychology." His article is valuable especially for its very sensitive sorting out of various degrees and levels of violence, or what he calls "secular evil." Diamond quotes Rollo May, one of the founders of humanistic psychology, who uses the term daimonic to describe a power or force that "can be either creative or destructive. … When this power goes awry, and one element usurps control over the total personality, we have 'daimonic possession' … this refers to a fundamental, archetypal

---

[5] Tom Mason, "An Archeology of the Psychopath: The Medicalization of Evil," pp. 103-104.

[6] Ibid., p. 107.

function of human experience—an existential reality."[7] The term "daimonic" is derived from Greek "daimon," meaning a powerful spirit that can inhabit us, can speak to us and inspire us, or possess us. Socrates consulted his daimon, for instance, when he didn't know what to do. Jung often speaks of his "daimon" as both creative and destructive. Like Jung, Rollo May speaks of it as an archetypal power. When this turns negative and destructive, or violent, it expresses the power of evil; when it favors creativity and constructiveness, it expresses the good. What still needs to be explained is why it turns one way or the other. Diamond suggests "severe narcissistic wounding" to be the cause.[8] This would seem to agree with the biblical account of Cain's violent rage against his brother Abel after having been narcissistically wounded by the Lord who rejected his offering.

Michael Stone, a professor of psychiatry and author of *The Anatomy of Evil*, offers a down-to-earth definition of evil similar to what the Supreme Court said about pornography: You know it when you see it. He writes: "Evil is a word answering to an *emotion*; specifically, the emotion of horror and revulsion when we hear of, or we witness, an action whose intention was to subject another person or group of persons to extreme suffering, extreme humiliation, degradation and, often enough, dehumanization. … There is something excessive, over-the-top, way beyond what can ever be accepted in the body social—in our usage of the word evil."[9] When we see this, whether in a film, on the streets, or in the news, we have a correspondingly violent emotion that

---

[7] Quoted by Stephen Diamond in "Violence as Secular Evil," p. 186.
[8] Ibid., p. 191.
[9] Michael Stone, "The Psychodynamics of Evil," p. 130.

elicits the word "evil." This is reflected in the etymological origin of the word. The word "evil" is a derivative from the Anglo Saxon *yfel*, itself a cognate of the German *über* and *übel*. *Über* means over, or beyond. It indicates in this case something that has gone over the boundary, over the edge. Stone, like Diamond, sees narcissism as the clinical backdrop of evil: "Since the essence of psychopathy as a diagnostic concept is a collection of narcissistic attributes, narcissism (usually in an extreme form) is the red thread that runs through the psychopathology we find in persons who commit evil acts."[10]

The philosopher Hannah Arendt, on the other hand, famously described evil as banal. In her New Yorker articles of 1963, "Eichmann in Jerusalem: The Banality of Evil," she describes her reaction to witnessing the trial of this mass murderer in 1961. Her term, banality, understandably caused outrage and controversy because it is the exact opposite of what most people felt about the genocide that Eichmann oversaw in the Nazi death camps. The whole Holocaust was reviewed in this very long trial, and it was sickening, horrifying. What springs to one's mouth is the word "evil," just as Michael Stone writes. If there ever was evil, this was it! Hannah Arendt sat there and listened through the whole thing. She came to a very strange and disturbing conclusion, She wrote: "Adolf Eichmann went to the gallows with great dignity… It was as though in those last minutes he was summing up the lesson that this long course in human wickedness had taught us – the lesson of the fearsome, word-and-thought-defying banality of evil."[11] This taught Hannah

[10] Ibid., p. 131.
[11] H. Arendt, *Eichmann in Jerusalem: A Report on the Banality of Evil*, p. 252.

Arendt the horrible lesson: the fearsome and thought-defying banality of evil. That phrase, "the banality of evil," stuck in the craw of many people. How can you say evil is banal when it's so excessive, so gruesome, so violent? When looking at Eichmann, who was one of the chief architects of the Holocaust, Arendt could see that he was drawn into a scheme as a bureaucrat, a rational man. In the shadow, however, he was power-driven and demonically possessed even as he carried out his duties with a cool spirit, organized, civil, legal, by the book. In the end, you could only say he's a banal man.

To think of evil in this way is something that we need to keep in mind, because evil isn't always theatrical and dramatic. It can be subtle, like the cunning serpent in the Garden of Eden. It can be enacted in a legally constructed system without breaking any written laws. One is doing one's civic duty, but one is serving something that is, at bottom, rooted in evil. This is quite different in appearance and emotional impact from what we might call radical evil, but at bottom it is no different. Radical evil is the counterpart to the banality of evil. Julia Kristeva, a French psychoanalyst, wrote an article on the website of the IPA (International Psychoanalytic Association) following the attacks in Paris that took the lives of many innocent people and shocked people around the world. Kristeva lives in Paris and was in the middle of the shocking destruction and violence. She's thinking about these attacks in Paris by radical Islamic fundamentalists when she writes, "What is radical evil? It is the declaration, and the realization, of the superfluity of human beings."[12] The mechanical destruction of "superfluous human beings" is what she calls radical evil. It is what Hannah Arendt, observing Eichmann on trial in Jerusalem, called the banality of evil.

On the Origins of Evil

Jung added a depth psychological dimension to consideration of the problem of evil in his designation of an aspect of the unconscious as the "shadow," the repressed part of human nature. The shadow has many levels and degrees depending upon what aspects of the personality are repressed. Shadow enactments of evil can range from relatively inconsequential motivations and actions all the way to enactments of radical evil (such as we see in personalities like Eichmann). Whether acts of radical evil are regarded as banal or astonishing by witnesses and judges is not important with regard to locating them on the spectrum. It is rather a question of unconsciousness. Shadow enactments of evil are by definition unconsciously determined. The more unconscious the motivation, the less emotion on the surface of consciousness.

In line with the level of consciousness described above as number 5, Jung as a modern man and psychologist located the agent responsible for evil motivation and enactment within the human personality and not in an external metaphysical agency like the Devil. Figures like Satan, or Dis in Dante's *Divine Comedy*, are considered to be symbols of psychological and not metaphysical reality. They are aspects of the shadow at an archetypal level of the

---

[12] http://kristeva.fr/interpreting-radical-evil.html

unconscious. Some aspects of the shadow lie at the fringes of consciousness, while others are located at a deeper level of the personality. Jung considered Freud's conception of the Id to be a fair description of important aspects of the shadow. These motivations and instinctual impulses are hidden from the conscious personality because of social conventions and feelings of shame and guilt that arise from their blatant enactments. The Id is an aspect of human instinct that is repressed for social reasons. Since the shadow is unconscious, shadow enactments are driven by motivations that that the actor does not and cannot acknowledge. When we enact shadow, we don't know clearly what evil we are doing and might feel quite innocent of evil intentions. Again, one can think of Eichmann's bureaucratic enactments of evil in carrying out the Holocaust under orders from above. It's only in retrospect, and reflecting deeply about what we've done, thought, or said from an ethical point of view, that we realize it was an enactment of evil that we have carried out unconsciously.

Jung asserts that the shadow has both personal and archetypal dimensions. He writes, "It is within the bounds of possibility for a man to recognize the relative evil of this nature ..." As Jung says, it's fairly easy to catch sight of this lighter feature of the shadow and perhaps offer apologies and make restitution. Jung continues this sentence, however, with "... but it is a rare and shattering experience for him to gaze into the face of absolute evil."[13] For someone like Eichmann to take on this level of responsibility for murdering millions of innocent people in the death camps would be shattering, indeed. And, of course, he did not do it. Nor do serial killers

---

[13] C.G. Jung, *Aion*, para. 19.

and child abusers. One is able to recognize the relative evil of one's nature because everyone is selfish, envious, hateful, and egotistical to a degree. However, "absolute evil" refers to another dimension, to the level of archetypal evil. To "gaze into the face of absolute evil" is to look into the abyss.

Jung gives these layers of shadow a quasibiological rendition in the following passage from *Mysterium Coniunctionis*:

> For just as a man has a body which is no different in principle from that of an animal, so also his psychology has a whole series of lower storeys in which the spectres from humanity's past epochs still dwell, then the animal souls from the age of Pithecanthropus and hominids, then the "psyche" of the cold-blooded saurian, and deepest down of all, the transcendental mystery and paradox of the sympathetic and parasympathetic psychoid processes.[14]

Absolute evil would be located in the "cold-blooded saurian" level. Dante's image of Satan, the figure named Dis in *The Divine Comedy*, is frozen in ice from the waist down. This level can be found, Jung writes, "if one is willing to risk one's skin to attain the greatest possible range of consciousness through the greatest possible self-knowledge—a harsh and bitter drink usually reserved for hell."[15]

For a mythological explanation of the source of evil, we can look at the biblical account in the book of Genesis. The

---

[14] C.G. Jung, *Mysterium Coniunctionis*, para. 279
[15] Ibid., para. 283.

Hebrew Bible offers a dramatic mythological account of the birth of evil in the world and locates its ultimate source in the Creator Himself. At the beginning of the Bible, we find an account of God's creation of the world and the creation of humans in God's image. This tells us something important: The nature of the human being is a reflection of the Divine nature. Looking deeply into the human soul, one sees the image of God. What can we deduce from this?

In the beginning, Adam and Eve lived in the Garden of Eden, a symbol of the self. Here they enjoy a state of preconscious wholeness, at one with everything around them and as unconscious as young children. In time, they develop some cognitive ability, including curiosity. There is a serpent in the garden, which God created and put there. "Now the serpent was the most cunning of all the beasts of the field that the Lord God had made."[16] The "cunning" of this beast suggests an advanced level of thought hidden away and latent in the unconscious. The serpent suggests a shadow thought to the mind of the feminine partner of the pair. It's a tiny temptation, just the beginning of a doubting thought. In Robert Alter's brilliant new translation of the Hebrew text, we read:

> And he said to the woman, "Though God said, you shall not eat from any tree of the garden—"

Eve interrupts and quickly tries to put aside this surprising thought emerging:

> And the woman said to the serpent, "From the fruit of the garden's trees we may eat, but from the fruit

---

[16] Genesis 3:1.

of the tree in the midst of the garden God has said, 'You shall not eat from it and you shall not touch it, lest you die.'"

The doubting thought continues despite this interruption:

And the serpent said to the woman, "You shall not be doomed to die. For God knows that on the day you eat of it your eyes will be opened and you will become as gods knowing good and evil."[17]

The myth shows a new level of consciousness emerging in the human mind. The ability to distinguish between good and evil arrives with the third level of consciousness (see above). The process of individuation attains this stage of consciousness when one becomes aware of the good vs. evil distinction among the various thoughts, feelings, and motivations that come into our minds. This is an essential development in the journey to conscious wholeness. Prior to this stage, one remains a child. The violent sociopath who feels no remorse and simply acts out impulses and emotional reactions displays the psychological level of a child's consciousness. Chronic episodes of narcissistic rage in an individual are a sign of this level of development.

Knowledge of the difference between good and evil is the precondition for the creation of the shadow in the personality. Prior to this, acts of evil are not motivated by unconscious agency because there is no division between conscious and unconscious. There is no need to repress feelings or thoughts because everything is allowed, as in a child's paradise. The

---

[17] Genesis 3:1-5.

psychological shadow is created when the ego identifies with what is known as the "good" and represses what is determined to be "the bad." At one level, the result of this operation is dependent on cultural habits and values in the surrounding milieu. A child eventually wants to be good and therefore pleasing to parents and other authorities and consequently cultivates and identifies with those agreed upon values. This is an early stage of moral development and involves distinguishing between good and evil as taken in from close relationships. The contrary impulses that are a part of the child's nature then get repressed and become unconscious. This becomes the personal shadow rooted in specific family and cultural values.

In the course of cultural history and ethical reflection, a list was established of the so-called seven deadly sins, which defined a general level of the shadow, the cultural level. These are: pride, envy, anger, sloth, avarice, gluttony, and lust. Pride is expressed as subtle or blatant narcissism in unconscious elitism, racism, or other attitudes of superiority; envy as unconscious acts of malice toward those we seem to admire; wrath as episodes of rage that knows no bounds; sloth as unconscious dependency on others and not wanting to carry one's own luggage; avariciousness as unconscious selfishness and absence of limits to one's desires for wealth and possessions; gluttony as unconsciously driven eating disorders like binging and vomiting and not being able to get enough to eat; and lust as unconsciously driven desire for sexual excitement and sado-masochistic pleasure. All of these show a degree of unmodified excess due to the lack of consciousness. This is quite a staggering lineup of shadow forces. In all of them, emotion dominates. Altogether they present a shadow mandala—the unconscious inner world of a one-sidedly virtuous, God-fearing person. Jung places this setup in his diagram of the Self in the Serpent Quaternio.[18]

This gives us a picture of the shadow forces we have to contend with in trying to be virtuous. Psychology has discovered that repression of them does not diminish their psychic power and energy, indeed the more energy that gets put into living one-sidedly for the opposing virtues (humility, mercy, peacefulness, solicitude, generosity, abstinence, chastity), the stronger the pressure becomes from the shadow side to act out. Shadow activity will be dramatically expressed in dreams and semiconscious fantasies. This can lead to enactments and acting out, when the grip of virtue simply evaporates in a cloud of unconsciousness. The other fact is that the repressed shadow aspects of the personality are projected into the environment, which then becomes contaminated with suspected evil motivations and intentions in others. The paranoia that results from projection sets the scene for violent confrontation and, at the level of nations, war. While virtue is claimed for oneself, evil is projected on "the others."

In many recent discussions of evil, violence has been located as one of the essential features in outbreaks of evil. As the biblical story continues following the expulsion of Adam and Eve from the Garden of Eden, we can see that consciousness of the difference between good and evil does not prevent violent enactment of shadow impulses. Emotions such as resentment and grievance can take possession of the individual and cause a kind of dissociation in the personality that leads to evil acts of murderous violence. We see in the story of the children of the First Parents, Cain and Abel. Cain

---

[18] See C.G. Jung, *Aion*, p. 231.

is an agricultural person, Abel is a shepherd, and both offer sacrifices to the Lord God. But the Lord does not deal with the sacrifices equally:

> And the Lord regarded Abel and his offering but He did not regard Cain and his offering, and Cain was very incensed, and his face fell.[19]

At that point, the Lord sees that Cain has fallen into a bad mood so he comes to his tent and counsels with him:

> "Why are you incensed,
> And why is your face fallen?
> For whether you offer well,
> or whether you do not,
> at the tent flap sin crouches
> and for you is its longing
> but you will rule over it."[20]

The shadow, envious rage, is crouching in wait for Cain. The impulse to express his violent anger is charged with emotion and eager to possess him. This is a vivid depiction of psychic reality: Sitting in his tent, Cain maintains his conscious position and can hear the good counsel of the Lord, but outside the tent in the unconscious shadow, his emotion waits to take possession of him as soon as he steps out. And it seems the Lord had overestimated his capacity to contain shadow energies, make them conscious, and refrain from enacting them. Cain has not developed that capacity

---

[19] Genesis 4:5-6.
[20] Genesis 4:7.

at this stage of his individuation, and he succumbs to the shadow.

> And Cain said to Abel his brother, "Let us go out to the field." And when they were in the field, Cain rose against Abel his brother and killed him.[21]

The biblical story shows the motivational source of violence. Envy, resentment, and bitter grievance boil up in Cain and lead to murderous rage that takes over the ego. This case is emblematic of violence throughout human history.

Throughout the Bible, this theme of the one who is privileged and preferred versus the one who is not—the chosen vs. the unchosen—runs like a leitmotif. Entitlement (pride) on the one side and resentment (wrath) are born out of this sign of preferential treatment on the part of the Lord. This theme features in many accounts of why people turn violent, why they commit acts of terrorism, why they become victims of the shadow sitting at the flap of the tent.

If one becomes unconsciously trapped in the shadow world as we see with people like Eichmann, for example, one creates a world made up of projections. A cocoon is spun around the ego-consciousness in order to preserve self-esteem and a sense of personal virtue, while the very shadow that one is enacting is projected onto the "other." This is the bizarre reversal of reality that one often sees in politics, where the side that is accusing the other of a particular type of evil is itself doing precisely what it is accusing the other of. The effect is to isolate the subject from the reality in the cultural environment. Instead of a true relation to the other,

---

[21] Genesis 4:8.

there is an illusory one. The outer world is painted in dark color. Shadowy unknown people are plotting evil all over the place. Projections change the perception of the world. They are the reflection of one's own unconscious shadow world. You are looking at your own shadow as you look out into the world and see all this evil coming at you.

Projection leads finally to an autoerotic or autistic condition in which one dreams up an ideal world whose reality remains forever unattainable. This present world is nasty and horrible, and the subject is the victim of evil forces in it. It is an unconscious factor that Jung calls the anima which, in consort with the shadow, spins the dark illusions that veil this world.

Conclusion

The Jungian discussion of evil took an important step further in the work of Erich Neumann's book *Depth Psychology and a New Ethic*. Neumann advocates for a new stage of ethical awareness that demands becoming aware of one's own shadow before making moral judgments. This sets a high standard, but it is in line with Jung's writings on the problem of evil. This would require reaching the fifth level of consciousness as discussed above. It's a much more difficult project than simply making up your mind to affirm good against evil, as Kant would have us do.

Blaise Pascal once wrote, "He who found the secret to rejoicing in goodness without getting angry at evil would have found the point. It is perpetual motion." This is the God-point, a state of being in motion without an external source of energy. Only God is beyond good and evil, but it is a goal of human individuation to maintain at least a semblance of balance when confronted by the opposites, even opposites as strong as good and evil. It's a matter of finding a point of equilibrium and gratitude for goodness even while investigating the shadow and something as dark and as dangerous and as off-putting and repulsive as evil.

Questions and Answers

Q: Is ISIS somehow different in its manifestation of apparent evil? Any thoughts on this?

Murray: If you look at instances of evil enactments—that is destructive, severely pathological, engaged enactments of destructiveness—I think that one could find many examples that are as vicious as ISIS. What ISIS has is basically an ideology that's based on some interpretations of Islam and a great deal of resentment and grievance. The ideology justifies the action, and the resentment generates the emotion. Most Muslims, by far the vast majority, reject these interpretations and these enactments. A lot of the people who join up with ISIS, young people especially, live in societies where they are in the second generation of immigrants. They may have many opportunities, even education and careers, but do not feel that their efforts are socially rewarded enough. I think you have a Cain and Abel story there. They are narcissistically wounded. This, in combination with some leadership and a lot of money and political influence, produces a phenomenon in the world, and throughout the world, that is bent on destroying anything that does not line up with a very narrow understanding of what is tolerable, with what is good in their eyes. In their definition of good and evil, we are the evil ones. They are the good ones, and they're destroying evil.

They are doing it with a huge vengeance, but that isn't so different from what many other ideologies have done in the course of history.

Q: In Jung's writings on good and evil, he says that the question of good and evil is largely a matter of human judgment. We don't know their essential nature. This distinction is a product of judgments we make. But then, in *Answer to Job*, he talks about the dark side of God, or the dark side of the self. If there is such a thing as the dark side of the self, is this not much more than a matter of human judgment?

Murray: I think when Jung pushes it to the archetypal level, he wants to say that evil is a part of the totality of the self, of a God image. He stays away from the question of God. It's the same when he's talking about archetypes. Are these ontological figures and forms? Do they have a standing beyond our conception of them, and our experience and images of them? Or are they simply products of the human mind? There is that tension in Jung as if he wants to sometimes say one thing and leans toward one side, and sometimes toward the other side. In his heart, I think he believed that they do have a basis beyond the human psyche, that the archetypes are rooted in nature, in the cosmos, and there is an archetype that we judge to be evil. But that is our judgment. I think he would say it has its roots somewhere darkly, deeply in the self, and also if it is in the self, there is no way to avoid it. That is one of Neumann's positions, finally, that you cannot avoid shadow enactments and evil enactments. It's built into the structure of the human. If you try to avoid it at all costs, you will live a very one-sided and neurotic life. Jung said at one point, it's not healthy to be too good. It tips you over. You increase the tension between two parts of yourself to such a degree that you're in a level of deep conflict with yourself, which is the definition of neurosis. The attempt to individuate and to achieve some semblance of conscious wholeness requires recognition, and even enactment knowledge, of evil. Knowledge comes about through experience and enactment. You don't know it deeply until you have experienced it, the shock of it. Sometimes you experience that in a dream, or you experience it in fantasy or in an emotion. You might not act on it, but you experience it deeply. Or you create an act of imagination as Jung did in *The Red Book*. That brings about the knowledge of it, which helps to ameliorate enactments of it. But I think Jung felt it's deeply woven into the nature of humanity and into the nature of the cosmos.

Q: I'd like to touch on Jung's concept that it's not healthy to be too good. What we often find in serial offenders is that when they try and overcompensate the good side of themselves and control that shadow side of themselves, they become unpredictable. That's when we see the level of violence rise.

Murray: That's very interesting. The criminal mind isn't so different from the human mind in general, just a little less balanced and more prone to extremes because of lack of developing the capacity to contain emotion—ego-strength we call it. Jung's cautionary statement has to do with mental health. It is better not to repress and project the shadow but to recognize it and integrate it. To try too be perfectly good leads to one-sidedness, repression, and neurosis.

Q: Why do you think humanity has succeeded in developing intellectually, that is creating all the current technologies that unite our world in extraordinary communications or sophisticated modalities of violence and destruction, and still we are seemingly stagnant when it comes to spiritual and emotional evolution, our inability to learn to love, to be compassionate, and so forth.

Murray: This is a question that I think about quite a lot. I've had many discussions with people about: Is the world getting better? Getting worse? Staying more or less the same in this regard? Personally, I think humanity is increasing in consciousness and the capacity to contain, but it is moving ahead with fits and starts. It seems that the development of social networks, which can also be demonized, can go either way—toward mobilizing the forces of evil, or mobilizing forces for good. In the end, our technological ability to communicate will make possible a kind of expanded consciousness on the planet among many people and not only the opinion leaders. That has the potential for uniting or dividing the world in a way it never has been before.

There are so many areas of life where ethics is now being discussed for the first time because of new inventions. For instance, in medical science, stem cell research is a big area. Other research areas, too, are raising questions from an ethical point of view, such as the creation and development of Artificial Intelligence. The fact that these questions are being asked is, in my opinion, an important step in raising consciousness. Humans will never solve all the world's problems and make it into a paradise. We're always going to have to deal with evil. It's written into humanity's code, but if we can simply continue the discussion and the reflection, inch by inch, it may bring about a greater consciousness. While we can't say the world is in a hugely more conscious place today than it was 1,000 years ago, I would rather live in this world than in that one. To live in a mythological age is not as promising for higher levels of consciousness as living in a scientific modern age where questions can be asked freely and discussed without immediate prejudice. I'm of the persuasion that while we've lost some valuable things in moving from a mythological to a scientific age, we can recover them in modernity through depth psychology. We can recover spirituality and a sense of meaning, which is most important. We can get it on another level, and I think that new level is much more promising for the future than all the regressive attempts to reinstate religions of the past. ISIS is a regressive attempt to go back to the seventh century. Fundamentalisms are all regressive attempts to retreat to premodern times. I don't think those are going to succeed, and I don't think they should succeed. I think there's another way forward, and I'm relatively optimistic about it.

References

Arendt, H. (1977). E*ichmann in Jerusalem: A Report on the Banality of Evil*. New York: Penguin Books.

Diamond, S. (2010). "Violence as Secular Evil." In T. Mason (ed.), *Forensic Psychiatry*. Totowa, NJ: Humana Press.

Frey-Rohn, L. (1967). "Evil from the Psychological Point of View." In *Evil*, edited by the Curatorium of the C.G. Jung Institute, Zurich. Evanston, IL: Northwestern University Press.

Jung, C.G. (1948/1967). "The Spirit Mercurius." In *Collected Works*, vol. 13. Princeton, NJ: Princeton University Press.

_____. (1951/1968). *Aion. Researches Into the Phenomenology of the Self*. In *Collected Works*, vol. 9ii. Princeton, NJ: Princeton University Press.

_____. (1955 and 1956/1963). *Mysterium Coniunctionis*. In *Collected Works*, vol. 14. Princeton, NJ: Princeton University Press.

_____. (2009). *The Red Book: Liber Novus*. New York: W.W. Norton & Co.

Mason, T. (2010). "An Archeology of the Psychopath: The Medicalization of Evil." In T. Mason (ed.), *Forensic Psychiatry*. Totowa, NJ: Humana Press.

Meloy, J.R. (2002). *The Psychopathic Mind. Origins, Dynamics, and Treatment*. Northvale, NJ: Jason Aronson.

Stone, M. (2016). "The Psychodynamics of Evil: Motives Behind Acts of Extreme Violence in Peacetime." In R.C. Naso & J. Mills (eds.), *Humanizing Evil: Psychoanalytic, Philosophical and Clinical Perspectives*. London and New York: Routledge.

The Symbolism of Evil
Religions, Myth, Fairytales, Film, Literature, and Dreams

Mary Tomlinson

I am a psychoanalyst and a lawyer. Justice has always carried numinosity for me. I'm going to be talking about the symbols of evil. That would lead one to ask: "What's a symbol, and what's evil?" I lean heavily on symbols emerging in human history. So, we have a wide and varied resource, covering many cultures, many modalities, many millennia. We're not just talking about evil; we're talking about symbols, which have their own numinous function, psychodynamically.

Meaning of "Symbol"

One person's symbol is another person's sign. In Jung's conception of psyche, the intensity of the symbolic impact depends on the particular person's "personal equation," as Jung termed it. The culture, the religion, the upbringing—a symbolic impact is a feeling, and it varies from person to person. Similarly, some things which come to my mind as evil may be totally different in your mind.

Symbols are subjective; they don't belong to theory. They're about how we actually feel when we see something, hear something, feel something. Although I've read many a chapter on evil, I keep coming back not to the concepts, but to the feeling, tone, images. They are the symbols of evil. Jung's early definition of symbol can be found in *Collected Works*, Vol 6.[1] It goes on for about five pages, so I just pulled out what I thought would be useful.

A symbol presupposes that the chosen expression is the expression of meaning. A symbol could be a cross, for instance. The cross is the chosen expression and is the best possible description, or formulation, of a relatively unknown fact which is, nonetheless, known to exist or postulated as existing. The living symbol is in part a conscious awareness, but it points to something in the unconscious, something serious, something we cannot conceptualize—the mysterious core of the symbol.

That living mystery is the *sine qua non* of Jung's conception of symbol. Every view, which interprets the symbolic expression as an analog, or an abbreviated designation for a known thing, is semiotics. Jung called it either a sign, or semiotic, when it isn't pointing to something in the unconscious. For Jung, the symbol is the best possible formulation of a relatively unknown thing, which, for that reason, cannot be more clearly or characteristically represented. He then, in the next paragraph, talks about the cross.

Jung uses the cross as an example of a symbol,[2] which over many centuries in the Christian world has, in his view,

---

[1] C.G. Jung, *Psychological Types*, paras. 814-829.
[2] Ibid., para. 816.

transformed into a sign. A symbol is a living thing pointing to an unknown mystery in the unconscious. That's what numinosity is—it galvanizes us, it catalyzes our very being. Only then is it a living symbol. Jung was well known to say that the Christian church's symbolic representation shifted from symbol to sign because it no longer held the numinosity that it did in days of the early Christian church. The symbol is alive only so long as it is pregnant with meaning. When Jung says feeling-toned, it means that you see an image accompanied by deep affect. And meaning comes along with that impact of affect/image.

But once it's meaning has been born out of it, once the expression is found, which formulates the thing experienced, seen, expected, or divined, it becomes a sign. Once we can formulate that which has heretofore been unconscious and mysterious, the symbol is dead. It possesses only historical significance. Note that it is impossible to create a living symbol. In other words, you cannot sit down at your desk and devise a living symbol. A living symbol comes out of our unconscious organically.

The reason is because a living symbol points to something unconscious, to a mystery. One can't sit here and formulate a mystery. That, by its very definition, is conscious. So, symbols come to us like Grace descending. We don't make them up. Physicist Dr. Adrian Beven says every scientific theory contains a hypothesis and is therefore an anticipatory description of something still essentially unknown.[3] Especially, with his interest in theoretical physics, the hypotheses within the theoretical sciences, to Jung, were symbols.

---

[3] A. Brevan, *Statistical Data Analysis for the Physical Sciences.*

Symbols state, or signify, something more and other than themselves, something that eludes our present knowledge. Whether a thing is a symbol or not depends chiefly on the attitude of the observing consciousness, on whether it regards a given fact not merely as such, but also as an expression of something unknown.[4] That's a really good summary of it, one that sort of nails it.

In his essay in *Man and His Symbols*, Jung uses symbol to differentiate between archetypes and instincts:

> The archetype is a tendency to form such representations of a motif—representations that can vary a great deal in detail without losing their basic pattern. …[Archetypes] are an instinctive trend, as marked as the impulse of birds to build nests, or ants to form organized colonies.
> Here I must clarify the relation between instincts and archetypes: What we properly call instincts are physiological urges, and are perceived by the senses. But at the same time, they also manifest themselves in fantasies and often reveal their presence only by symbolic images. These manifestations are what I call the archetypes. They are without known origin; and they reproduce themselves in any time or in any part of the world …"[5]

Elsewhere, Jung described archetypes not as something occurring in time and space, but as energy *in potentia*. Their manifestations in time and space are called archetypal images, not archetypes. I think it's important to note that

---

[4] C.G. Jung, *Psychological Types*, para. 818.
[5] C.G. Jung (1964). "Approaching the Unconscious," 67-69.

throughout his works Jung differentiates between archetype per se, which exists outside of the psyche, and archetypal image, which is the manifestation in the psyche of the archetype per se.

A manifestation of symbols of evil possesses a feeling tone that is numinous and takes the conscious mind on a deeper search. It moves the conscious mind emotionally through its numinosity into a deeper experience of something unknown. It can fill the observer with awe, and fear, and fascination.

Symbols of evil can arise in fairy tales, myths, literature, fiction, poetry, film, the media, and human history, past and present. They can arise in dreams and fantasies, which Jung called natural symbols, or they can become part of a particular collective culture, which Jung called cultural symbols. Again, the important thing is they are not consciously made up. That's why people love their dreams—they have no conscious part in creating the symbols, but the symbols are theirs.

In *Man and His Symbols*, Jung says that an archetype, or archetypal motif or image, like a hero myth, originated in a period when man did not yet know that he possessed a hero myth, in an age when he did not yet consciously reflect on what he was saying. The hero figure is an archetype which has existed since time immemorial, before man was self-reflective. He just carried it out naturally, because our archetypes are the framework of our being.

I suggest that the archetype of evil also comes to us despite our post-Enlightenment minds and continues to exist in our collective unconscious, even though we know there aren't any devils or ghosts "out there." It's an ancient image emanating from our unconscious. It continues to exist in the collective unconscious, there to be constellated by the present time and place. Archetypes are the core of any complex and the core of symbols. As such, symbols can exert possession over consciousness.

Symbols, unlike archetypes, don't have a universal impact. Like Jung's example of the "cross," the symbol is representative of a particular country, culture, religion, or spirituality. It can vary in impact between individuals—one person's symbol can be another person's sign, the latter meaning an image that points to something fully known, fully conscious.

A manifestation of the symbol can be an image, like the cross. It can be a famous quote or a saying. It can be archetypal plot, or motif, such as the hero's journey. It can arise out of nature. It can be a character in a particular piece of fiction. It can be a song. I tried to think of what songs stir us, and of course, this comes from my own personal equation. But the biggest ones I could think of were "Ave Maria" and "Jerusalem." Everybody has other songs that put the hair up on the back of their necks. Speeches like the Martin Luther King's "I Have a Dream" and "I Have Been to the Mountaintop" are words that have become a part of the African American heart. A relationship can be symbolic, like the symbolic relationship between mother and infant.

The symbol has the potential to constellate a huge amount of psychic energy in the observer, to the extent that it synthesizes the opposites in that person's psyche, conscious and unconscious, and transforms them both. It allows for the integration of at least part of the dark mystery of the unconscious. Jung calls this dynamic the transcendent function. By being conscious, or at least more conscious, the archetype loses some of its ominous, dark, projective impact on consciousness and the external world.

Meaning of "Evil"

Now that we have a handle on "symbol," we can ask: What is meant by evil? Is it sin? Is it the devil? Is it anything that is taboo? But that doesn't sound strong enough. It has to be excessive. Taboo is not excessive. Sleeping with your cousin is just not enough over the top to qualify as evil. Is evil an entity, floating in the ether, waiting for a human to be taken over by it, to be its conduit? Or is it better described as a part of all human beings, their darkness, that may or may not be constellated in their life to varying degrees? For this presentation, I have spent time wandering among images of symbols of evil in its many manifestations. Gradually, sone patterns emerged.

One way to describe a culture, historically or anthropologically, is through its symbols of evil and how they compensate the collective consciousness and reflect the collective shadow. Older civilizations simply assume the existence of evil. They're not post-Enlightenment. One could also trace their symbols of defense against evil to determine the nature of their unconscious darkness, symbolic figures like ferocious gargoyles outside of temples. Someone, maybe 500 years from now, might think that North America's symbols of defenses against evil consist of superheroes. That's how we ward evil off. We create superheroes.

I tried to organize and categorize the manifestations of evil through the collective symbols and our strong feelings about what is right and wrong, what is good and evil. The U.S. Supreme Court Justice Potter, regarding the definition of pornography, refused to define it due to its infinite manifestations but said: "I know it when I see it."[6] I think there's something of

---

[6] https://en.wikipedia.org/wiki/Jacobellis_v._Ohio

that to evil. We know it when we experience it. The function of symbols of evil is to make our darkness light, to integrate shadow into consciousness, and to take moral responsibility for shadow rather than project it out into the world.

What occurs to most people when they think of evil is that they think of the intentional infliction of suffering and death on others for the sake of power, rage, revenge, enjoyment, or even because it's their job. The Nazi swastika symbolizes this kind of evil. Hannah Arendt, in her book *Eichmann in Jerusalem*, coined the phrase "the banality of evil." As she watched the trial, she saw that Eichmann displayed neither guilt for what he had done nor hatred for those trying him, claiming he bore no responsibility for participating in acts of atrocity toward Jews because he was just doing his job. This kind of enactment of evil often requires of the perpetrator a loss or absence of empathy, a dissociation or a split within and without. If you have empathy, it generally stops you from wanting to hurt somebody. Eichmann's psychological examiners found him to be neither monster nor sociopath as we usually understand these conditions, but rather a balanced rational personality simply following orders from above. This suggests we're all capable of such actions.

Six Categories of Evil

Categories of evil contain overlapping symbols, but the numinous, feeling-toned impact on the observer will be its own individual life experience.

The first category features the image of the scapegoat.

The second involves the projection of the negative feminine, which includes the classic symbol of the witch, the evil stepmother, and the devouring mother.

The third category is the projection of the negative masculine, which features brutal and excessive violence and destruction. This we find in Joseph Conrad's novel *Heart of Darkness* and in a film about the war in Vietnam, "Apocalypse Now."

The fourth category I find is the evil of taking away someone's will or sense of self or soul. The body remains. We didn't kill the body. We have killed the soul. That, to me, is a form of evil. It might include the Faustian bargain with the Devil, where Faust sells his soul to the Devil for power and knowledge here on Earth. It also includes images of the invasion of zombies and vampires and werewolves on TV and movie screens. This is a manifestation of fears that have been pushed down into the unconscious because we're so post-Enlightenment. They come up in another way. Everywhere you look are movies and TV series about these creatures or people from outer space who will take away your mind. How many clients have analysts seen who were not allowed in childhood to bring their own selves into being, sentencing themselves to lifelong suffering? That is what gets constellated in the face of this kind of evil, where your self and your soul have been taken away from you.

The fifth category is evil as sin. In any particular religion, sin means going against the essential tenets of God's laws as interpreted by humans. In Islam, sin treated as evil can see a woman stoned to death for adultery. In Christianity, sin can be forgiven. During the Inquisition in the 15th century, sin could amount simply to not being a Christian, and Jews who did not convert to Christianity paid the price. In the 16th century, the Pope declared that South American indigenous people have no souls and, as such, the invading Conquistadors could rape, torture, and kill with impunity because they were not contravening God's laws. Two-thirds of the indigenous population in South America was wiped off the face of the Earth, which was not considered a sin, not considered evil.

Finally, the sixth category is "chaos versus order," the former being the evil in this duality. Chaos and order have symbolized evil and good in many contexts and cultures. I tried to think of something chaotic, violently chaotic. I thought about the sacking of Rome, but I also suggest Picasso's painting "Guernica," where we abandon all hope in the face of chaos.

More on the Categories

The unconscious, and especially one's shadow, cannot be seen or known directly, only indirectly through projection. The darkness in us has found its way into the outside world and has hurled itself self-righteously at the hook for that projection in order for us either to confront our shadow or for our ego-consciousness to split shadow off, not to know or to take responsibility for it. By not recognizing and integrating our own shadow, a great deal of evil has been perpetrated throughout human history.

An ancient iconic symbol of this phenomenon of unconscious projection of shadow is well-known today as the scapegoat, an innocent victim of a wrongful projective assault, who must bear the sins of the individual or of the collective so that collective can be protected from fear and shame. The origin of the scapegoat comes from many ancient cultures, which attests to its universality. In the Judeo-Christian tradition, it stems from a practice described in the Old Testament, where a goat was chosen for this function and driven out into the desert bearing the sins of the community upon him. This was a ritual to cleanse the community and relieve it of guilt. I quote the Bible: "… and Aaron shall cast lots upon the two goats, one lot for the Lord and the other lot for Azāzél. And Aaron shall present the goat on which the lot fell for the Lord, and offer it as a sin offering; but the goat on which the lot fell for Azāzél shall be presented alive before the Lord to make an atonement over it, that it may be sent into the wilderness to Azāzél."[7]

Sending Out the Scapegoat, by William Jay Webb

---

[7] Leviticus 8-10.

Another instance of projection of evil, this time again onto animals, is told in the New Testament (Mark 5:1-20), when Jesus is shown to come across a man on the road who was full of unclean spirits. He is mad and has been possessed by devils. In modern-day parlance, we would call this mental illness and give him a psychiatric diagnosis, perhaps paranoid schizophrenia. Jesus draws the unclean spirits out of him, and as he does so, the devils ask him to send them into the nearby herd of swine. Until I read this again, I didn't realize that the devils asked Jesus to put them in the swine. I just thought there was this handy nearby herd of swine and that's where Jesus cast them. But now it seems to me that Jesus, in this event, plays the role of projector of the shadow. He removes it from the person and throws it into innocent pigs who suicidally hurl themselves off of a cliff into the sea. I suggest that is a picture of what we're doing when we take our darkness and we put it onto somebody else, somebody who's innocent, and we punish the person for that. We can't bear seeing our darkness, so it must be that person's. We are freed from it, and that person suffers.

Murray Stein: This really gets into them. I would like to just reflect on this for a moment, Mary, because Jesus doesn't punish the pigs. The pigs go mad. They take in the projection. That's the other side. If evil is projected onto you, you end up behaving accordingly. You take it in. This happens, for instance, in families all the time. The scapegoat does become the misbehaving kid. It's like it's accepted. It's projective identification. You receive the projection, and it affects your psyche and your identity.

Mary Tomlinson: It definitely affects your sense of self if you are the hook and you live up to it or down to it. And not only does the person projecting not realize they're projecting, but also the person receiving doesn't realize they're receiving. It's actually seen in transference and countertransference within the analytic partnership. That one's unconscious is acting on the other's unconscious such that the analyst starts to behave accordingly. It's an unconscious projection taken in by the analyst. We could say that Jesus Christ was the biggest scapegoat of them all. He was crucified for the sins of the world, all the sins of the world, all the darkness. He was crucified so that the world could be freed of sin and guilt and enter the Gates of Heaven.

Murray Stein: He was innocent like the goat. All the sins of the community are placed upon it, and it is driven out into the wilderness and dies. Thus the community is cleansed by this ritual. It's clear in the biblical narrative that Jesus accepts the role of the scapegoat. This is his myth. He is living his myth. It's quite conscious for Jesus, which is different from the goat who most likely does not understand what's going on when it's put in this role.

Mary Tomlinson: When Jesus was in Gethsemane, he said "take this burden from me," but he knew it was his destiny. "I don't want the sins of the world on me, but that was the deal," is what this says to me.

Murray Stein: A problem with the scapegoat solution to shadow problems is that while it does offer temporary relief from a sense of shame and pollution, this is because the shadow is projected out and not consciously worked through. So the problem returns in a short while. The projection has to be repeated. You have to find a new scapegoat. You can't just do it one time. In psychotherapy, we try to make the shadow conscious and take responsibility for it. This is a very different solution.

Mary Tomlinson: But if we don't do this work, it does come back. It can come back in even worse evil form if it's never integrated. Which brings me to my next scapegoat—the African American. The African American in the U.S., especially the South, is another scapegoat carrying the projection of shadow—the dangerous Other with a black skin, the opposite to White. They came to receive all of the hatred and rage of men who had become powerless and needed to find their only power in persecuting the black man because they could.

The ancient Greeks had a similar ritual—they called their scapegoat "*pharmakos*," the Greek word for "medicine" or "charm," from which we get our word "pharmacy." This was a ritual that instead of using a goat used a slave, a cripple, or a criminal, who was expelled from the community at times of disaster like famine, invasion, or plague.[8] It was believed that this would bring about purification. On the first day of the Thargelia, a festival of Apollo at Athens, two men, the *pharmakoi*, were led out as if to be sacrificed.

Purification took place on the first day of the festival, so that the town and townspeople could make a fresh start. One or two human scapegoats were chosen for their ugliness (or other undesirable qualities). Those figures, known as *pharmakoi* (singular *pharmakós*, feminine *pharmakis*), were draped with figs, fed, led in procession through the city, whipped with vegetation (so as to transfer impurity to them), and driven out. Occasionally, as in times of heavy calamity, plague, or the like, the *pharmakoi* were sacrificed, usually either thrown into the sea or burned on a funeral pyre. Sometimes the *pharmakoi* were merely expelled from the

---

[8] https://en.wikipedia.org/wiki/Pharmakos

city. On the second day of the festival, there was a thank
offering, a procession, and the official registration of adopted
persons.[9]

Scapegoats are selected based on certain qualities or
features and then sacrificed for the sake of the community's
health and well-being, whether religious or secular. Looking
at well-known human scapegoats in history, we see that they
most often are the Other, people who are alien, foreign, or

---

[9] https://www.britannica.com/topic/Thargelia

simply unknown to the prevailing collective consciousness and, as such, receive the projection of the shadow. The unknown is threatening to people. The unknown Other stirs our unconscious fears. They are labeled dangerous and evil. The most massive and long-running history of shadow projection and objects of scapegoating are the Jews, in Europe from the 12th century to today. Ghettoized as early as the 14th century in Florence up to the ultimate evil of the Holocaust, they are the objects of Europe's collective paranoid, rage-filled projection.

This is a photograph from Auschwitz showing a wagon full of bones and skulls with witnesses standing by.

Umberto Eco, a well-known Italian semiologist and philosopher, wrote a novel about 18th- and 19th-century conspiracy theories in Europe entitled *The Prague Cemetery* about how the Jews surreptitiously took over the culture they lived in and subjugated the non-Jews. It is a book about a conspiracy theory, about the Jews being evil. This is one of the last books he wrote before he died. Eco wrote a wonderful mystery about 12th-century monks being mysteriously killed—*The Name of the Rose*. So I naturally ordered his next book and found that I couldn't continue reading it past the first few chapters. It seemed to take the soul right out of me. It was fiction, but he had done all the research, and it was based on actual reality. He researched all of the theories about why the Jews were evil. He started with Prague, but he then went to France. They were thought to be running a secret international conspiracy oppressing the collective for its ultimate ruination. Reading the book, I felt overwhelmed by the paranoia and projection that can take over a collective and the harm that it can do.

The Witch is another familiar projection, this one of the negative feminine. This is an image of a scapegoat in the form of the evil woman, from Lilith in the Garden of Eden to witches and midwives in the Middle Ages and beyond. During the 15th-century Spanish Inquisition, women were thought to be witches, causing evil to men by seducing them or casting spells on them through their closeness to nature. It is said that over a few centuries, six million women were burned at the stake or otherwise executed because they were considered to be witches.

Fairy tales have given us the negative feminine as symbol of evil in the wicked witch and the evil stepmother. The latter reflects the splitting of the mother into a good mother and a bad mother. Melanie Klein describes this as an early phase of ego development, the paranoid-schizoid

position.[10] This is the position of infants, according to Klein, when they cannot see that both the good comforting breast and the bad or withholding breast belong to the same mother, and, therefore, they split them into two opposites. This is a position of people who cannot see reality as both good and bad at the same time. Klein's "depressive position" occurs when the infant is finally able to bring the opposites together in one mother. We do not see this in the fairy tale because the fairy tale's function is to reflect the unconscious and not the conscious synthesizing of good and evil. It's to delve into that dark part of the psyche where you find the negative feminine. The wicked witch is probably it's most famous symbol.

In modernity, the wicked witch made an iconic appearance in "The Wizard Of Oz," which came out of

---

[10] M. Klein, "Notes on Some Schizoid Mechanisms."

Hollywood in 1939. It still scares children and adults today. There was a rapt fascination with the symbol of the wicked witch pitted against the hero's journey, atypically the feminine hero being Dorothy with her red shoes. When I was a child watching it, I can remember I had to run out of the room when the wicked witch came on the TV screen, she scared me so much. Then her flying monkeys just did me in. My parents would have to tell me when it was over so I could come back in. That's what the wicked witch/negative feminine does. She scares you to death. She terrorizes you.

As with all archetypal symbols, there's both a positive and a negative manifestation. In "The Wizard of Oz," there was the positive feminine in the good witch Glinda. She's dressed in a white gown and sparkling crown and wand with blond hair and a voice like a babbling brook. She helped the protagonist Dorothy who was trying to get home, accompanied and supported by three animus aspects—the tin man with no heart, the scarecrow with no brain, and the lion with no courage. She was also accompanied by her supportive, loyal, friendly instinct, her little dog, Toto. The good witch helped them to see that home, heart, brain, and courage had been in them the whole time. They simply had to realize it. It wasn't "out there." It's in you. You just have to bring it into consciousness. That's the good witch. Glenda's opposite, the Wicked Witch of the West, was green, haggard, bent over, dressed all in black with a tall, black witch's hat with a cackling, threatening voice that I can still hear today saying, "I'll get you my pretty and your little dog too." That's the devouring negative feminine.

Many works of fiction and film have traced a kind of possession that took over Salem, Massachusetts,[11] such that people were convinced that some women were witches especially if they were young and attractive. It has been termed a case of Colonial America mass hysteria which possessed the people and surrounding communities. It was attributed to isolationism, extremist religion, false accusations, and lapses in due process. Nonetheless, it was about the demonizing of women as it had been since the 15th century. In one year, 20 people were executed, 14 of them women. A recent film to come out of Hollywood was entitled simply "Witch." The reviews said the movie is fantastic, and the really important thing is that the audiences are scared to death. It contains no obvious cackling wicked witch with a black pointy hat. Yet the audiences found it so terrifying and horrifying that they

---

[11] https://www.britannica.com/event/Salem-witch-trials

had to pull back or leave. It's a story of one family's frightful unraveling in the New England wilderness in 1630, just prior to the Salem Witch Trials. Upon threat of banishment by the Puritan Church, a father and mother and three children flee to a remote plot of land on the edge of an ominous forest in which, in their imagination, there lurked an unknown evil. It is a deeply unsettling portrayal of paranoid torment and repression and projection in an isolated Puritan family. The oldest daughter was or was not a witch. You, the audience, have to come to a conclusion or experience the blackness and whiteness of it, which apparently was scarier than the witch from "The Wizard of Oz." The oldest daughter was or was not a witch, and the unfolding fear of the parents and the children formed projections that the oldest daughter was willing to take on. She was willing to be seen as a witch. She liked the power it gave her. The audiences were so scared! As Jung said, these archetypal images of evil don't disappear just because we possess a post-Enlightenment consciousness that doesn't believe in anything it can't see, touch, or measure.

The witch is nature's personified feminine. She's often a little old woman out in the forest. Sometimes, like all symbols, she's the good old woman who helps, but sometimes she is not. She draws her powers from her closeness to nature. In fairy tales, she's usually found in the woods in a little cabin. She invites the power of nature to do her bidding, for good or for evil. With her magic spells, she can possess you, your consciousness, your very being, put you to sleep for a hundred years, or take your place as a false bride. The evil and the fear it invokes is in being possessed by the will of the other.

That is the deep fear: being possessed by the will of the Other. In this case, it is the negative feminine. This symbolic possession finds its equivalent in the psyche in states of possession by negative complexes. Intention and will mean nothing. They are puny compared to the possession that a complex can execute. A stark example of this possessive power manifests in the anorexic who brings herself to the brink of death because she sees only a fat person in the mirror. That is the power of the complex possessing the conscious mind.

Think of the OCD sufferer who is trapped in a spell of compulsive behavior as if in a prison that can't be willed away. Such possession is an ongoing torture from which there is no escape, as if you're under a spell. Is it any wonder the symbolic fairy tale figure who can possess your very soul has a numinous feeling tone of evil? When the wicked stepmother and the wicked witch are split-off opposites from the good witch and the good mother, evil can prevail because they're not connected or synthesized. The good and the evil are not brought together. They are split apart. No compensation or integration into consciousness can take place, so shadow remains evil in its projections.

The fairy tale is not telling you what the right thing is. It is telling you what is in our dark unconscious. In North America and the U.K., there exists the Wicca religion. It is a religion, and the adherents say they are witches and warlocks, but the good kind. They're the white witches. Their ritual and their devotion are to Mother Nature. This positive connection to nature is a deeply held conviction of spirituality, and it is the opposite of evil.

The devouring mother is another form of the negative or dark feminine. As a child, a sense of separation can be collapsed by an overwhelming mother whose ego boundaries merge with that of the child's. I think of this as evil, and every analyst sees in the consulting room. It can cause suffering with little joy even unto death. There's a loss of freedom and personal agency, since the child's ego-consciousness is enlisted into the service of the narcissistic devouring mother.

My client, "Alice" (not her real name), now in her 70s, had a mother who would brook no unique personality in her daughter. The daughter was her co-narcissist who had to pack away her own sense of self to offer up what her mother demanded of her. Her father was not strong enough to intervene. "Alice" is now fervently on the trail of her own unique self, but she rarely remembers her dreams, so I asked her to engage in an active imagination that involved her mother and herself as a child. Two weeks later, she brought me a collage. It was not a painting because she said it was too scary to get that close to her mother. It was a collage of magazine pictures that gave her some distance. In the foreground, inside a large mouth, was my client's picture, an actual picture of her as a little girl. It took my breath away. I had never once used the phrase "devouring mother" to "Alice." Also in the mouth there were little pictures of items that her mother had taken away from her. She'd go to school, and when she'd come home, her bike wasn't there, or something else would have disappeared—things that mattered to her. The mother told her, "Oh don't be silly, you don't need them," even though they were precious to her. Her very sense of self was in that mouth.

The wicked witch of "Hansel and Gretel" in her candy house in the woods is another example of the devouring feminine. The fairy tale is an example of the devouring feminine, but she's not a mother; she's a witch. Hansel's and Gretel's mother doesn't exist in the tale. They have a stepmother, and the father and the stepmother put them out into the forest because they couldn't afford to support them. The fairy tale splits the good mother and a stepmother because we cannot conceive of a good mother abandoning her children.

Murray Stein: The German analyst Hans Dieckmann wrote about the use of fairy tales in analysis. He talked about the wicked stepmother as the negative side of the mother, and as you said, the mother is split into good and bad. There's a good mother, and there's a bad mother. In a sense, we all have that experience. Part of our mother is good, and part of our mother is bad in our eyes. The bad one doesn't understand us and is not on our side.

Mary Tomlinson: And it's always a matter of degree, isn't it? For this particular client, she spent the rest of her life trying to piece together a self. That collage for me was chilling. In the iconic movie "Psycho," Norman Bates is the adult son who owns the family motel. He talks to his mother throughout the movie, and every time a pretty woman rents a room, his mom tells him to kill her because of course, it's the competition. It's like "Snow White." The negative, devouring mother requires her son to kill off any woman who is potential competition. Norman's mother has devoured his ego-consciousness. He does her bidding. In fact, the psychologist at the end of the film (Norman is eventually caught) determines that Norman no longer exists as a personality. The mother has taken him over completely. The scene of Norman stabbing a woman in the shower is symbolic both of the possession of Norman by his negative mother complex but also of the rage of being possessed. Just so you know, he talks to his mother throughout, and the viewer sees profiles of Mother throughout. Then you learn at the end of the movie that mom has been dead for decades. He sat her in the rocking chair, this being her chair, and looking out the window.

Murray Stein: Do you think films help us know the psyche better by giving us these images and symbols? In other words, do they perform a therapeutic function in the sense that they bring out of the dark the various dynamics and hidden contents and give them image?

Mary Tomlinson: I think that depends on the movie. In this movie, there was a psychologist at the end who said his personality had been taken over by the mother. That I think people can relate to and see the results when it's in the extreme. But there's an awful lot of movies that have such gratuitous violence and misogyny. I don't think you are facing your shadow that way—you are rather living it out vicariously without collective consequences. People are drawn to it. People are fascinated because it's shadow.

References

Arendt, H. (1963). *Eichmann in Jerusalem. A Report on the Banality of Evil.* New York: Viking.

Brevan, A. (2013). *Statistical Data Analysis for the Physical Sciences.* Cambridge: Cambridge University Press.

Dieckmann, H. (2013). *Twice-Told Tales. The Psychological Use of Fairy Tales.* Asheville, NC: Chiron Publications.

Eco, U. (2011). *The Prague Cemetery.* New York: Houghton Mifflin Harcourt.

Jung, C.G. (1964). "Approaching the Unconscious." *Man and His Symbols.* Garden City, NY: Doubleday & Co. Inc.

_____. (1971). *Psychological Types. Collected Works*, Vol. 6. Princeton, NJ: Princeton University Press.

Klein, M. (1946/1986). "Notes on Some Schizoid Mechanisms." *The Selected Melanie Klein*, edited by Juliet Mitchell. New York: Viking Penguin Inc.

The Holy Bible. Revised Standard Version. New York: Harper & Row.

The Atom Bomb and Our Collective Confrontation with Evil

Valerie Appleby

I am casting my eyes over pictures of the artwork in my grandfather's house, sent to me by my mother. Do I want to "put my name" on any of it, she asks? Among the images, four stand out with solemn prominence: large, faded photographs of nuclear tests overseen by my grandfather. In one, a stark and savage bloom of light mushrooms up from a desert valley, in colors shifting from black to red to blinding white. Each of the others shows a ball of light hovering above the Pacific Ocean, like a *fata morgana* of technical prowess—a manmade sun. The edges of the pictures are somewhat blurred and faded, as if the very fabric of reality has been distorted by the blasts they depict. Looking at them, I feel awe, and terror. I cannot easily look away.

I want them.

"Everybody wants them," my mother later confirms. "We'll need to get copies made."

I guess we all want to claim this bit of family history. We all want to own it, even as we fear and despise it. Even as we despair over it. Even though it is not something that we need to claim. It is our birthright.

The Sins of the Father

> *Wilt thou forgive that sin where I begun,*
> Which was my sin, though it were done before?
> *Wilt thou forgive that sin, through which I run,*
> And do run still, though still I do deplore?
> —John Donne, "Hymn to God the Father"

In the most *bombastic* language, my grandfather is a mass murderer. Of course, this is not strictly true, but it helps to weave the story. For 40 years, he was a nuclear physicist and weapons designer at the Los Alamos National Laboratory—home of the Manhattan Project. There, his remit was to perfect weapons of mass destruction, including atom bombs of increasing sophistication, and even hydrogen bombs.

One might imagine such a man to be somber, if not stricken by guilt and remorse; hot-tempered, if not aggressive and violent. Yet these qualities have never been prominent in my grandfather. Nearly always, they have remained buried, as nuclear waste. But that waste, while remaining largely out of sight, may nonetheless have had a contaminating effect.

If every explosion is accompanied by an equal and opposite implosion, then my grandfather's psyche must be holding a lifetime's worth of highly radioactive material—material as destructive as the bombs he created. What has become of that waste? And what are its implications—for him, for his offspring, for myself? For humanity?

Although most nuclear waste facilities can be located with minimal effort, they remain some of the most highly guarded places on earth. As I have come to know more about my grandfather's history, I have noticed the reticence with which he speaks about his experiences; how quick he is to change the subject. And yet, those large photographs of the bomb remain prominent in his home.

I have learned not to ask him too many questions. Instead, I have taken to looking at those photographs, allowing them to pull me into their deep mystery. I have come to embrace them as one might embrace an enigmatic dream, seeking meaning amidst their complex layers— scientific and historical, symbolic and archetypal.

This chapter summarizes the state of my exploration to date: one that weaves through personal and historical material to unveil the symbolic and psychological meaning of the atom bomb, and what it may teach us about evil—both overt and "banal"—for which we must all take responsibility.

Sol Niger

As my attention began to turn to this aspect of my family history, I had the following dream:

> *I am in an airport, gathering as many bottles of sun protection cream as I can carry. I do not know why I am doing this, but I somehow sense that it is very important. Later, I look up and see a black sun in the sky, flanked by two black angels, with wings covering their faces. I shudder in horror, knowing that, at some point, the angels will reveal themselves, and I may not be able to survive their stare.*

I woke up shaken, wondering: Can any amount of SPF protect me from those dark angels? From the black sun?

Like many Jungians, I have a personal interest in astrology as a symbolic language through which to explore human personalities and world events. I was curious about the black sun in my dream, and wondered if astrology might offer me some clues to its interpretation. Guided by an intuition that the dream was commenting on my relationship to my family history, I drew up the astrological birth charts of my paternal line. Immediately, I noticed a striking pattern: a conjunction between the sun and Pluto. A dark sun. It was present in my own chart, as well as those of my grandfather and great-grandfather. With each generation, the aspect had grown in strength: mine was strongest—nearly exact—in Pluto's domicile of Scorpio.

Scorpio. The unearthing of taboos. Could it be my destiny to unearth Pluto's dark destructiveness within my ancestral line? To bring it to light? Might this dark energy be strongest in myself? Stronger than it was even in my grandfather? Is it safe to touch?

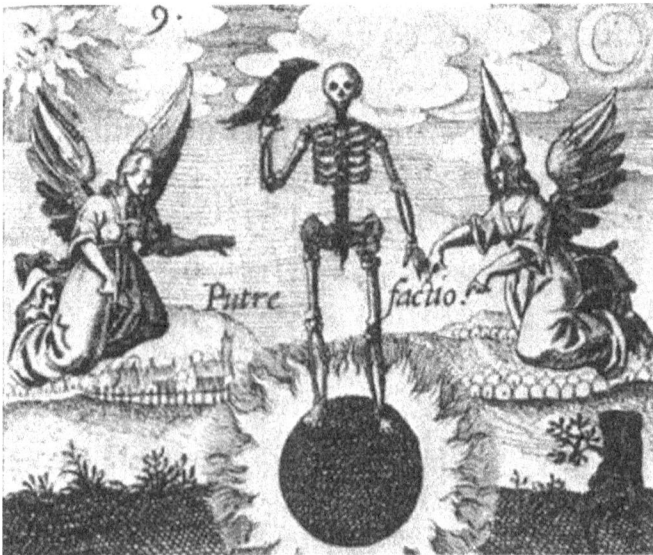

Source: C.G. Jung, *Symbols of Transformation*, illustration 34: 'The *nigredo* standing on the *rotundum*, i.e., *sol niger*. —Mylius, *Philosophia reformata* (1622).'

I note that the sun was also conjunct Pluto when the bombs were dropped on Hiroshima and Nagasaki.

It is no great mystery why my psyche might have presented my nuclear inheritance—or the encounter (or potential encounter) with my ancestral shadow—as a black sun, or *sol niger.* To Jung, the *sol niger* was an important image of the alchemical process of the *nigredo*, characterized by the confrontation with the shadow. His conceptualization drew on an extensive alchemical literature, from which he borrowed a variety of terms, including *"putrefactio, mortificatio,* poisoning, torture, killing, decomposition, rotting, and death."[1] A more literal description of the consequences of the atom bomb would be difficult to find.

But my dream was not pointing to the bomb in its physical capacity, but to its psychic reality in myself. This was an equally terrifying prospect.

There are two ways in which we may confront the shadow: one is through critical self-reflection and the other—more common—is through encounter in the world. Looking at the Pluto-sun conjunction on the days the bombs were dropped, it is easy enough to see the collective shadow that was unleashed on the world, with horrific consequences. Surely, it would have been better for humanity if the destructive potential of the shadow had been integrated *within*. But who among us is capable of withstanding that degree of psychological torture, even when humanity, itself, is at stake?

Nonetheless, this is the demand of the *sol niger.*

As the natural sun emits light, so too must the *sol niger* have its own particular dark illumination. Perhaps,

---

[1] S. Marlan, *The Black Sun*, p. 11.

we might come closer to this shadowy psychic mystery and the terrifying wisdom it contains by exploring the atom bomb's physical properties and processes, and their potential symbolic correlates.

The Promethean quest

If two hydrogen atoms collide with enough force, they fuse together to create helium, a spare neutron and a great deal of energy. This process, known as *nuclear fusion*, is the physical process that powers the sun. Fusion is not an easy process to replicate in the lab and, to date, it has never been achieved with any efficiency (that is to say, until very recently, the amount of energy needed to fuel the process has always exceeded the output). Part of the reason for this difficulty is that, for hydrogen atoms to collide, they must be moving extremely quickly. And this requires tremendous heat, in the realm of 200 million degrees centigrade.

Despite some recent scientific breakthroughs, nuclear fusion remains a utopian dream. If achieved, it would change the trajectory of climate change, ensuring a habitable planet for ages to come: the fuel it requires (hydrogen) is virtually limitless, and the end product (helium) is harmless and "clean." Nuclear fusion is the perfect way to make energy, but seemingly impossible for humans to achieve. And should it not be so? After all, it is the energy of the sun, the fire of the gods.

But we humans have a Promethean streak. And it may still be our fate to steal that fire—or at least to die trying.

In the 1930s, scientists discovered that, while nuclear fusion may be a pipe dream, *nuclear fission* was entirely achievable as a method of producing energy. Unlike fusion, which forces the collision of smaller nuclei, fission works by splitting larger nuclei. While both processes create energy, their methods are entirely opposed: the nuclear fusion of the sun is self-generative, natural and virtually limitless; while fission is technological, highly energy intensive and limited by the extent of its input materials. Additionally, while fusion relies on the lightest, safest and most abundant elements in the universe, fission requires some of the heaviest elements, which are radioactive and toxic, also in their byproducts.

Indeed, fission is no substitution for fusion. And while its discovery may have satisfied a bit of our Promethean urge and will to power, allowing us to "create" and release huge forces of energy, the question remains: How should this energy be evaluated? Is it equivalent to that produced by the sun, or do these energies have distinct qualities?

The Matter of Life and Death

A look at the raw materials may reveal some crucial insights. The sun—the greatest power cell in our universe and the source of all light (and life)—is fueled by the simplest and most abundant atom in the universe: hydrogen. Hydrogen is the material from which all other elements are created; in this vein, it may symbolize the fundamental building block of the psyche, from which all consciousness stems. Its atomic make-up of a single proton and single electron represents a fundamental unity and the potentiality of opposing forces, evoking the primal energy or creative force that gives birth to consciousness. It is undifferentiated, raw material, lacking in identity. However, its tendency to fuse with other elements makes it creative of new compounds, reflecting the process of psychological integration and individuation.

The end product of fusion, helium, is an exceptionally light gas with the property of buoyancy—suggesting the movement of psychic contents closer to consciousness. Within medicine, helium is used in combination with oxygen to improve breathing and reduce airway resistance. In this way, it supports life, as well as the capacity for ingestion (i.e. knowledge, logos) and communication (i.e. connection, eros). Furthermore, as the second lightest element and one of the main components of stars, it may symbolize the potential for transcendence and spiritual transformation.

Thus, we may describe the energy of solar fusion as that which is conducive to consciousness. Of note, it is an energy that relies mainly on eros (fusion), but produces logos (conscious awareness). Even current efforts to achieve fusion in the laboratory are reliant on an extraordinary degree of international collaboration that is rarely seen in any research discipline.[2] In fusion, matter is combined into more than the sum of its parts.

Fission, naturally, requires elements that are heavy enough to split. For this purpose, two elements are used: uranium and plutonium. If hydrogen shows a tendency to fuse into helium and rise to the surface, then uranium and plutonium show the opposite tendency—to sink and scatter. Merely touching an atom of uranium or plutonium with a single neutron will split it in two. This will liberate a huge amount of energy (approximately one billion times more than that which is generated in a typical chemical reaction) as well as a couple of neutrons, which will then hit two more

---

[2] In contrast, the development of nuclear fission occurred within the context of a world war and global arms race, under conditions of unparalleled secrecy.

nuclei to cause a chain reaction. This chain reaction will liberate an exponential amount of energy (e.g. an explosion), which will only subside when the supply of uranium or plutonium is exhausted.

How might we think about this, psychically? Heavy contents should naturally reside below consciousness; that is to say, in the unconscious. And these particular contents are so highly radioactive that they may spontaneously fissure, generating energy autonomously. This suggests that the contents may lie particularly deep in the unconscious, as Jung describes that the deeper, less differentiated contents of the psyche have the greatest tendency to act autonomously. Uranium brings to mind the myth of Ouranos—the tyrannical father of the gods who ate his own children. In this vein, it may symbolize the negative masculine in its most archaic, destructive form, as well as the enantiadromic tendency towards its own annihilation (much as Ouranos spawned the agent of his own undoing). Perhaps, the weightiness of this element is also symbolic of the tremendous psychological burden that accompanies the destruction of the "father" (e.g. our cultural artifacts, civilizations, mindsets, etc.) that is often necessary for individuation—both collective and individual. Indeed, astrologically, the planet Uranus is associated with the potential for innovation and breakthrough, via rebellion with the current order.

Uranium is the heaviest *naturally* occurring element in the universe, while plutonium is synthetic—produced in technical refineries from slightly decayed uranium. This suggests that nuclear fission, understood psychically, may have both archetypal and personal roots. Plutonium, as a synthetic element, is formed by human actions and experience. In line with this, the planet Pluto is associated (astrologically) with the shadow aspect of the psyche, which holds repressed, disowned and unknown parts of the self—in this context, perhaps parts that collude with the negative masculine, in its tyrannical or destructive aspects.

The role of uranium and plutonium in nuclear fission reminds us of the immense power and potential for destruction that can arise from psyche's deepest layers. If such power is unleashed autonomously, it is likely to issue a painful destruction of conscious structures—exactly opposite to the sun's symbolic creation of consciousness. Of course, however unwelcome this destruction may be, it will always carry the potential for spiritual transformation.

Interestingly, the process of nuclear fission was discovered by two scientists: a female physicist, Lise Meitner, and a male chemist, Otto Hahn. (However, Meitner's contribution was largely elided in the historical record when the Nobel Prize was awarded only to Hahn.) At the time of their discovery, they anticipated that the science would be used to create nuclear reactors. These reactors, which would be safely contained in water, would be used to turn steam turbines, generating energy that was conducive of life and living. Thus, the addition of a feminine element (i.e. water) could be used to transform the energy produced by nuclear fission into something qualitatively more similar to that produced by the sun. Ultimately, this vision became a reality. But not before the science was first applied to create a weapon of mass destruction the likes of which the world had never seen—an artifact of negative masculinity in its most pure, physical form.

The Creation Story

> *Do I dare*
> *Disturb the universe?*
> —T. S. Eliot, "The Love Song of J. Alfred Prufrock"

In 1940, two Jewish refugee physicists at the University of Birmingham, Rudolf Peierls (German) and Otto Frisch (Austrian), sought to uncover how much uranium-235 (U235) would be needed to create an explosion. The answer frightened them: a chunk of U235 the size of a grapefruit would be enough to create an explosion equivalent in strength to 1,000 tons of conventional explosives.[3] On top of this, the explosion would produce radiation. They published a memo about this "super bomb," claiming: "As a weapon the super-bomb would be *practically irresistible*. There is no material or structure that could be expected to resist the force of the explosion."[4]

At the time, it was not known whether scientists in Germany had already reached the same conclusions. Was Hitler building this weapon? The only defense against that scenario would be for the UK to beat him to the punch.

What is the likelihood that, during this stage of the war, these two Jewish refugees had uncovered sizeable chunks of uranium in their own psyches that were threatening to erupt in acts of existential violence? Do we not often see victims acting out the role of persecutor? Could it not have been this very psychic material that even triggered their investigation into the precise "recipe" for the bomb? Luckily, there is no

---

[3] G. Farmelo, *Churchill's Bomb.*
[4] Emphasis added; Frisch and Peierls, "The Frisch-Peierls Memorandum."

evidence that these scientists acted out any such violent or destructive urge. Rather, they noted an urgency and reflected on the science, and this may have been sufficient—and necessary—to prevent any autonomous fission of the volatile uranium within.

Conveniently, the scientists—as well as their host nation, the UK—had a common enemy on which to project their will to violence and destruction: Hitler and his armies. Certainly, if the UK got the bomb before Hitler, they could determine the outcome of a war they looked ready to lose. Thus, a top-secret project was initiated under the code name "Tube Alloys."

In America, a similar project was encouraged by Albert Einstein (himself a Jewish refugee) in a letter to President Roosevelt, written in the summer of 1939. The letter alluded to the possibility of explosives, but was speculative.[5] Nonetheless, on the basis of the letter, Roosevelt initiated a research project to determine feasibility. After the bombing of Pearl Harbor, funding ramped up and the project was transferred to the Army Corp of Engineers, which had a virtually limitless budget and the capacity to manage a top-secret project of incredible complexity. The project was thereby named the "Manhattan Project."

Although the Manhattan Project involved hundreds of manufacturers across all US states, the majority of the work was conducted at three sites: Oakridge (Tennessee), where centrifuges were used to produce enriched uranium (i.e. U235); Hanford (Washington), where reactors and facilities were used to produce plutonium; and Los Alamos (New

---

[5] A. Einstein, "Letter to President Roosevelt."

Mexico), where the scientific research laboratory and design center was based. This is where my grandfather worked.

The first atom bomb, known as the "Trinity," was produced within 24 months. It was tested just before dawn on 16 July 1945, in a desert of New Mexico known as the "*Jornada del Muerto*" (or "Journey of Death"). No one knew what would happen. General Leslie Groves, who was leading the project within the Army Corp of Engineers, prepared three statements for the New Mexico governor, in advance of the test: the first indicated that the test had been successful; the second announced severe damage; and the third included the obituaries of all present, including himself.[6] Neither he nor the scientists involved knew the true power of the forces they were playing with—the energy they were unleashing. They only knew that it would be destructive, to some degree. Groves' three statements reveal a modicum of humility in the face of this terrifying unknown, yet an equal—if not greater—degree of hubris, through his decision to move forward with the test.

When the bomb went off, the flash in the sky was described as "brighter than a thousand suns," with "night turned instantly into day." Although the scientists who were present were 20 miles away, they reported that the heat was scorching, like that of an "open hot oven." This all occurred in the space of an instant. Five minutes later, the sound reached them, like thunder echoing in the mountains all around. A mushroom cloud rose 20,000 feet in the air, changing color as it pushed into the sky.[7]

---

[6] R. Rhodes, *The Making of the Atomic Bomb*.
[7] R. Jungk, *Brighter than a Thousand Suns*, pp. 201–202.

The test was considered successful, and the scientists were in awe. They had controlled and liberated the energy of the atomic nucleus. They had given birth—though to what, they were not sure. The implications were not yet clear. What was clear, however, was that the nuclear age had just begun.

Within three days, Enrico Fermi, one of the Associate Directors at Los Alamos, announced in a lecture that the heat from an atomic explosion would be hot enough to spark a hydrogen bomb[8]—a bomb so devastatingly destructive that there could be no credible military justification for its use. The Trinity test had seemed to confirm and celebrate the power of "man," the power of science, and the power of these particular scientists in New Mexico, opening their eyes to possibilities so technically enticing that they were blind to the need for a moral imperative. Peierls and Frisch's prediction of an irresistible super-bomb was proving true.

It is difficult not to read a will to power—and particularly an omnipotent, divine power—in the scientists' quest. The very name of "Trinity" ascribes a spiritual ambition to the technology (if not a divine proclamation, altogether), leading us to understand the bomb as a symbol for the power of god, brought into man. In fact, the name of the bomb was inspired by a poem by the English poet John Donne, "Batter My Heart, Three Person'd God."[9] Oppenheimer, who was the Director of the Los Alamos National Laboratory, understood this "three person'd God" as a great force that could compel humans to do good. Similar to Prometheus, who hoped that the fire he stole from the gods would benefit humankind,

---

[8] Ibid, p. 374.
[9] P. Templeton, "Plutonium and Poetry."

Oppenheimer believed that this weapon of death would be redeeming, by ending the war.[10]

While I do not wish to suggest that Oppenheimer was necessarily wrong in this belief, the record suggests that he was defensively chained to this fantasy, holding that "it was the duty of the scientists to build the bomb, but it was the duty of the statesman to decide whether or how to use it."[11] His outlook was famously rooted in the *Bhagavad Gita*, and especially the dialogue between Arjuna and Lord Vishnu about the importance of upholding one's dharma, despite emotional attachments, in order to maintain the cosmos and society. While Jung interpreted this passage as Arjuna's entreaty to Vishnu to free himself of the splitting of opposites (cf. fission) and thereby pursue his individual dharma,[12] Oppenheimer instead seems to have interpreted his dharma as one that was entirely imposed on him by the collective—and therefore split from more personal, unconscious dimensions, whose consideration would precede a moral reconciliation. And at what price? One of the most famous lines attributed to him is said to have been spoken after the Trinity test, when he quoted the *Gita*: "Now I am become Death, the destroyer of worlds."[13]

If Prometheus was strong enough to carry the tension between the human and the divine (in his suffering of the punishment for his theft), Oppenheimer seems to have fallen short of this standard. But his self-emancipation from the moral suffering implied by his work (i.e. his splitting), under the guise of scientific "duty," may have been necessary,

---

[10] R. Jungk, p. 572.
[11] Hijiya, in P. Templeton.
[12] C.G. Jung, *Symbols of Transformation*, para. 253, n4.
[13] P. Templeton.

as the suffering required—the confrontation with the *sol niger*—was likely more than what any individual could bear. Nonetheless, the suffering could not have been avoided, and if it did not take place consciously, then it was necessarily lived out neurotically (i.e. unconsciously), through projection and its consequences.[14]

It is not my intention to suggest that Oppenheimer, Groves or any of the scientists involved in the Manhattan Project were necessarily "wrong" to create the bomb; only in their apparent tendency to split scientific progress from moral deliberation. As Jung wrote:

> Ultimately everything (particularly in the case of the atom-bomb) depends on the uses to which these factors are put, and that is always conditioned by one's state of mind. The current "isms" are the most serious threat in this respect, because they are nothing but dangerous identifications of the subjective with the collective consciousness. Such an identity infallibly produces a mass psyche with its irresistible urge to catastrophe.[15]

We might say that, when armed with such a powerful technological instrument as the atom bomb, Oppenheimer was misguided to identify too strongly with collective ideologies (i.e. the "dharma" of scientific progress) and belief systems (i.e. the US must beat Hitler to the bomb and "rescue" the world from war), as this may have driven him to destructive

---

[14] We might even consider the later loss of public/political trust in Oppenheimer during the McCarthy era through this lens.
[15] C.G. Jung, *Structure and Dynamics of the Psyche*, para. 426.

actions, motivated by unconscious impulses and complexes (e.g. a deep-seated desire for power, chaos or control). Had Oppenheimer had the psychological maturity to confront these difficult impulses, the bomb may have taken a different shape, or been used in a different manner. But it would have taken a person of extraordinary strength to stop the military-industrial machine driving the Manhattan Project, and to resist the tremendous prestige on offer. Lest we forget: the atom bomb that was living through Oppenheimer—splitting his psyche into convenient and not-so-convenient pieces— was a "super-bomb" that was "practically irresistible."[16]

Nonetheless, some tried to resist it: 153 of the scientists involved in the Manhattan Project signed a petition that urged President Harry S. Truman to carefully consider what it would mean for the US to be the first country to drop an atom bomb. But the petition never reached Truman or the Secretary of War. General Groves stamped it as classified and locked it away in a safe, presumably operating under a similarly fragmented understanding of the situation.[17] Thus, the US proceeded with their planned military operations in Japan, dropping the first atom bombs on the cities of Hiroshima and Nagasaki.

The bombs claimed the lives of 140,000 in Hiroshima and 74,000 in Nagasaki. An equal number were injured. Major portions of both cities were flattened. In the weeks, months and years to follow, nuclear radiation caused thousands more to suffer from radiation sickness. Survivors are known as *hibakusha*, and they continue to suffer from lifelong psychological trauma. Many are still plagued by

---

[16] R. Frisch and O. Peierls.
[17] R. Jungk, p. 749.

anxiety. They do not know when their symptoms of radiation sickness may occur. Their foremost wish is that no one will ever experience what they have gone through.[18]

In his 1945 essay "After the Catastrophe,"[19] Jung discussed the psychological impact of the atom bomb on the collective unconscious. He argued that the bombing of Hiroshima and Nagasaki caused a profound shift in the collective psyche, leading to a sense of existential fear and uncertainty that was unprecedented in human history. He also noted that the bombing had exposed the limits of human rationality and the dangers of unchecked technological progress.

In subsequent writings, including his 1957 book *The Undiscovered Self,* Jung expanded on these themes, arguing that the atom bomb coincided with a profound shift in human consciousness. He suggested that the bomb had shattered the illusion of human control over the natural world, revealing the potential for human self-destruction and the need for a new sense of ethical responsibility and spiritual awareness. Maybe if one person—Oppenheimer—could not carry the ethical responsibility for the bomb, collectively, we might have a shot.

As one example of this collective task, due largely to the efforts of the *hibakusha*, on 22 January 2021, the UN Treaty on the Prohibition of Nuclear Weapons came into force. Currently, there are 92 signatories, including the world's largest nuclear stockpilers, the US and Russia.

---

[18] International Campaign to Abolish Nuclear Weapons, 'Hiroshima and Nagasaki Bombings.'
[19] C.G. Jung, *Civilization in Transition*, paras. 400–444.

Tending to the Split

Despite Lise Meitner and other women's crucial contributions to atomic science, women were largely uninvolved in the actual weapons development of the Manhattan Project, and instead relegated to roles as nurses, librarians and secretaries.[20] It is interesting to imagine what might have been different had women been more directly involved in the weapons' research and design. Likely, the work would not have resulted in atom bombs named "Fat Man" (the bomb dropped on Nagasaki) or "Little Boy" (the bomb dropped on Hiroshima). If the Trinity bomb can be considered a physical manifestation of the power of god brought (in warped form) into man's hands, then Little Man and Fat Boy subsequently directed that power in a total assault on nature—a rape, of sorts, penetrating the earth, its cities and its peoples and violently splitting them to pieces, both physically and psychically. When the bombs were dropped on Japan, their pure masculine energy burst into the world, leaving a purely feminine condition of chaos in their wake. Neither of these states can be said to be particularly comfortable.

The bombs' mechanism of destruction, characterized by a chain reaction of splitting, evokes René Girard's description of violence as tending towards an endless chain of revenge acts with the potential to decimate a community. Girard depicted such violence as characteristic of our earliest ancestors, who were seemingly as easily "caught" by the archetype of the negative masculine as the scientists in Los Alamos. In Girard's telling, sacrificial violence may be

---

[20] A. Lantero, 'How Women Helped Build the Atomic Bomb.'

instated to interrupt this chain and restore harmony. But for the sacrificial violence to be effective, the sacrificial victim must sufficiently resemble the endogenous targets, yet stand outside the community, so as not to incite further acts of revenge.[21]

It is perhaps controversial, but not without solid grounds, to suggest that the bomb, itself, had the potential to serve as an agent of sacrificial violence, with the aim of ending the cycle of violence that characterized the Second World War. While the primary motivation for the Manhattan Project was to beat Hitler to the bomb (and to defeat Hitler, more generally), the bomb was not dropped on German territory, but on Japan: a nation that resembled Germany (as an ally) but stood outside it. Furthermore, the mechanism of the bomb resembled the ever-expanding chain of violent war acts that had resulted in a growing World War. And indeed, the historical consensus is that the dropping of the bombs on Hiroshima and Nagasaki effectively ended the war. Thus, those two acts of incredible violence led to a previously unimaginable entreaty towards peace.

Allowing this hypothesis to stand does not, however, resolve the guilt of the executioner. Girard explains that those who perform the act of sacrificial violence must purify themselves, in order to prevent further violence. This purification serves both to cleanse the actors of their sins and to rid them of any further impulse towards aggression.

Did the politicians and the scientists involved in the Manhattan Project purify themselves, or did they simply content themselves with burying the "waste"? Without a doubt, the historical record suggests the latter. Had they

---

[21] R. Girard, *Violence and the Sacred.*

publicly (and convincingly) atoned and suffered for their war crimes, perhaps the act of dropping the bombs would not have led to an era of nuclear proliferation and the constant threat of nuclear war—in itself another chain reaction of violence, simmering just beneath the surface.

In *On Violence*, Hannah Arendt argued that violence is ultimately self-defeating, as it always leads to more violence. Drawing on the case of the atom bomb, she held that its use was counterproductive, as it created a culture of fear and distrust that perpetuated a threat of global destruction. To her, the atom bomb was a symbol of humanity's ability to destroy itself (a point on which Jung agreed). She further claimed that the focus on technological progress and the pursuit of power had led to a neglect of the ethical and moral considerations that should guide human actions.

We might suggest that Girard's perspective contributes a spiritual read of the situation, while Arendt focuses more on feeling—both of which appeal to me strongly. However, Arendt's claims rest on a counterfactual that is impossible to predict: could the war have ended via anything but violent means? And if so, how many more lives would have been suffered and lost before this end was reached? Similarly, Girard's perspective raises important questions: If the "guilty" parties in the bombing had appropriately purified themselves after their act of violence, would the scientists, politicians, and all of mankind have been cleansed of the moral detritus, into the future? Or is nuclear waste an inevitability? Furthermore, is any individual truly capable of purifying themselves of such an act, or is this a burden that must be shared amongst the wider collective, and even future generations?[22] Who must be held accountable?

Evil and Accountability

In 1956, Oxford University announced its intention to award an honorary degree to US President Truman, in recognition of his leadership during the war and his contributions to shaping post-war international relations. In response to this announcement, a young female philosopher, Elizabeth Anscombe, published a public letter in *The Isis*, Oxford's student magazine.[23] In the letter, Anscombe eloquently laid out her opposition to Oxford's decision, arguing that Truman's authorization of the use of atom bombs during the war, despite a full awareness of the civilian lives at risk, was morally unjustifiable and tantamount to an act of murder on a massive scale.

Anscombe's letter sparked significant controversy and generated widespread attention, both at the university and internationally. While her protest failed to prevent Oxford from conferring the degree, it was successful in stoking ethical discussion around Truman's decision. It also laid the groundwork for Anscombe's influential philosophical treatise *Intention*, which she published the following year. In *Intention*, Anscombe outlined a new virtue ethics of moral responsibility centered on (conscious) intent. She argued that an evil act is one that is committed with a *deliberate intention* to bring about harm or wrongdoing; and when this

---

[22] The question of who suffers most from nuclear waste—both geopolitically and psychically—is an important one that merits deeper investigation, but is beyond the scope of this chapter.

[23] G. E. M. Anscombe, "Mr Truman's Degree."

intention for harm or wrongdoing is present, an individual can be held accountable for their actions.

This frame of thinking about evil, which we find at the basis of most criminal codes and jurisprudence (i.e. *mens rea*), seems basically agreeable. But does it go far enough? Does our responsibility truly extend only so far as our conscious understanding, knowledge and intent? If so, this would be psychologically comfortable—not to say convenient. But of course, when we begin to consider the influence of unconscious motivations on actions, the assignment of moral responsibility becomes more intricate, and requires broader ethical and psychological considerations.

The question of whether or not we are responsible for our unconscious impulses is difficult to tackle head on. There are evil impulses that we are blind to because they are rooted so deep in the collective unconscious, and there are evil impulses that we are intentionally blind to, as a result of repression, denial or avoidance. And even the deepest, darkest sources of evil are likely to rise through, amplify and express themselves in line with those shallower, shadow contents, for which we bear some responsibility. So it is to those contents that we must turn, in order to continue this exploration.

Elsewhere in this volume, Stein and Tomlinson make reference to Hannah Arendt's famous description of evil as "banal"—an insight she reached while observing the trial of the high-ranking Nazi official Adolf Eichmann.[24] Arendt's elaboration on this point provides a necessary corollary to Anscombe's framework: evil deeds emerge not solely from malevolent intentions, but also from thoughtless obedience

---

[24] H. Arendt, *Eichmann in Jerusalem*.

and a lack of critical and moral self-reflection—a splitting of the Self. We observe such splitting when individuals conform to societal norms and obey authority figures unquestioningly, while suppressing their own ethical judgment. And of course, Eichmann was not alone in this endeavor; did not Oppenheimer also find some escape in his "dharma" of scientific duty?

At this point, we have considered two frameworks of evil: one that is active and defined by conscious intent (i.e. "overt" evil); and another that is defined by a privation of ethical or spiritual reflection—that is to say, a failure to engage in deep and critical evaluation of one's actions and their potential motivations and consequences (i.e. "banal" evil). Importantly, banal evil does not imply blamelessness. Rather, it suggests that we have a moral responsibility to contemplate the impact of our actions on others and their broader consequences for society. It challenges us to recognize that evil deeds can emerge not only from conscious malice, but also from thoughtlessness, indifference and blind adherence to external influences. Moreover, it alerts us to our tendency to justify or rationalize our actions based on ideological, cultural or societal norms, even when those actions may result in serious harm. Such rationalization may serve as a defense mechanism, shielding us from a more honest and complete survey of our innermost motivations, and the ethical reckoning these may demand.

From this perspective, profound ethical contemplation allows us to maintain—and even strengthen—our integrity, providing a critical safeguard against the inadvertent perpetration of evil acts. In contrast, defensive splitting in order to avoid uncomfortable self-reflection makes us smaller and weaker, while simultaneously strengthening the destructive potential within and the shadow projections without. This process is aptly illustrated by the atom bomb, with its endless splitting resulting in maximal destruction.

Of course, the atom bomb reflects splitting (and destruction) in the extreme; but extreme cases have pedagogical value. On an everyday level, we split our consciousness on a smaller scale, causing varying degrees of harm to both ourselves and others. In modern parlance, we apply the word "evil" to only to the most extreme acts of harm and cruelty. This select usage, meant to underscore the immense gravity of certain acts, is both useful and meaningful. Nonetheless, I would like to suggest that, perhaps, evil is not defined only by its menace, but also by its method—a method that is quite banal and commonplace, and difficult to avoid. A humbling thought, indeed.

Frankenstein's Monster or Chernobyl's Dog?

I dream that I am in a spooky, large, dark house, with my father, mother and brother. The space is round and vaulted, like the center of a cathedral. I look up to the ceiling and see what appears to be a human body hanging from a noose. My family and I walk up a staircase that winds in a spiral along the inside of the building. At the top, there is a small balcony that circles the perimeter, like a whispering gallery. From there, we can see that what's hanging from the ceiling is not a human body, but a monstrous creature: a white dog-human hybrid. My father and mother rejoice. Their experiment has worked! They have successfully created the world's first dog-human, using my blood, my genes. The animal is half me. Although it's hanging from the ceiling, it is not strangled. Quite the contrary, it has more than its fair share of energy. It attempts to devour me, starting with my hands.

This dream positions me in the shadow—that dark, spooky area of the psyche. A place of death, or at least the allusion to it. A hybrid creature—part dog, part human—has been made from my blood. My genes. And now I've come face to face with it, this creature of Frankenstein, this product of science. As my parents rejoice over their scientific creation, the monster eats away at me. I wonder, did my grandfather consider what the work of his hands threatened to destroy? What his participation in unchecked scientific and technological process might threaten, on a creative and spiritual level? Did he not recall that Frankenstein's monster ultimately caused the deaths of the creator's friends, family and fiancée, and eventually himself? That the threat of the monster only disappeared when he jumped into the sea?

But many things thrive under the sea, waiting for an encounter to lift them up.

And nuclear waste remains dangerous for thousands of years, even when buried 655 meters underground.

In this dream, I've found it. The nuclear waste. Part of the *sol niger* I have been tasked with facing. And I know how dangerous it is.

A few minutes after waking from this dream, I receive a push notification on my phone from the *New York Times*. An article has just been published describing a population of dogs in the exclusion zone surrounding the Chernobyl nuclear power plant. The dogs are the descendants of the pets that were left behind by their owners during the evacuation following the nuclear disaster in 1986, a mere 6 months after my birth. The dogs are mongrels, but their DNA most resembles that of German Shepherds, Rottweilers and boxers. Over time, the dogs have adapted to life in the contaminated environment.[25]

The dream seems to be calling me to learn about my own "Chernobyl dog"—that dog living in the "exclusion" zone of my psyche. This particular dog seems content to destroy me, just as a Rottweiler, German Shepherd or boxer is apt to react to an intruder. But it is also the product of my lineage, just as the Chernobyl dogs are the product of nuclear disaster. Do we all have such a beast within us?

In the dream, the dog-human attempts to devour me— eating my hands, compromising my creativity. Its energy is overpowering. It needs to be trained. It contains all of the destructive tendencies and instincts of the atom bomb, and it is now my task to tame it.

I enter into Google: "How to train a Rottweiler to make it less aggressive." The results tell me that the dog must be socialized (slowly exposed to a variety of people, environments and situations) and put through obedience training (to sit, stay, come and heel). If it is already displaying aggressive tendencies, the training is more difficult and time-consuming. It is important to be patient, and consistent.

But how can I train a dog that is currently eating my hands? How can I get (back) the "upper hand"? How can I make this dog my companion and protector, rather than a monster set to devour me?

---

[25] E. Anthes, "In Chernobyl's Stray Dogs, Scientists Look for Genetic Effects of Radiation."

I am struck by its pure, white color. The Iroquois tribe, local to the area of America in which I grew up, believed that white dogs were messengers of the Creator. This dog may be carrying a vital message. Despite its light appearance, it may be holding the wisdom of my black sun.

Nuclear Waste

To deactivate a nuclear device, one must know the exact sequence in which the pieces were originally put together, in order to reverse the process. If this goes wrong, there is a possibility of accidental detonation (at worst), or exposure to nuclear and other toxic chemicals (at best). Once the weapon is dismantled, one must then deal with the leftover uranium or plutonium. Under certain conditions, these elements can be repurposed to create electricity; but mainly, they are stuck in storage, where they decay according to a half-life that ensures their toxicity for millions of years.

The things we fail to acknowledge and atone for fall into the shadow—our personal shadow, our collective shadow and, in my case, my ancestral shadow. There, they continue to contaminate us—to eat away at us, or to explode into the world, in ways we may not even recognize, let alone intend.

As Jung (1964) described in his essay on "Self Knowledge," the atom bomb within us is our tendency to split our consciousness, letting through what we deem tolerable while excluding everything we deem intolerable about ourselves. It is precisely this tendency that creates the conditions for banal evil. While the shadow that is created in this act of splitting is, by definition, in our blind spot, we can—and must—take up the work of unpicking it: unpicking the process, by becoming aware of our fissile tendency, and unpicking the material that this tendency has split off—the nuclear waste. We must continuously work towards deactivation—de-nuclearization—and perhaps even introduce the element of water (i.e. grace, compassion), for additional safety along the way.

The work is indefinite. Both personally and collectively. In my psyche and in the world, the atom bomb remains existentially dangerous and nuclear waste continues to accumulate. This chapter represents only one small attempt at outlining the responsibility and work required to remedy this course and prevent a nuclear disaster of the sort presaged in the film *Oppenheimer*: a succession of explosions, with the world turning black.

My analysis has not arrived at a destination, nor does it presume to have travelled far along the precarious path. If the bomb is too large a responsibility for any individual to hold, it remains too large also for me. But it may be my destiny to face it—to look into the eyes of those dark angels around the black sun—and suffer them as best I can. I invite you to join me in this quest.

References

Anscombe, G. E. M. (1958). "Mr Truman's Degree." *The Isis*. Available at: http://www.ifac.univ-nantes.fr/IMG/pdf/Anscombe-truman.pdf

Anthes, E. (2023). "In Chernobyl's Stray Dogs, Scientists Look for Genetic Effects of Radiation." *The New York Times*, March 3. Available at: https://www.nytimes.com/2023/03/03/science/chernobyl-dogs-dna.html

Arendt, H. (1963/1994). *Eichmann in Jerusalem: A Report on the Banality of Evil*. New York: Penguin Books.

_____. (1970). *On Violence*. New York: Allen Lane.

Donne, J. (1633). "Holy Sonnets: Batter My Heart, Three Person'd God." Available at: https://www.poetryfoundation.org/poems/44106/holy-sonnets-batter-my-heart-three-persond-god

Einstein, A. (1939). "Letter to President Roosevelt." Available at: https://www.atomicarchive.com/resources/documents/beginnings/einstein.html

Eliot, T. S. (1915). "The Love Song of J. Alfred Prufrock." Available at: https://www.poetryfoundation.org/poetry-magazine/poems/44212/the-love-song-of-j-alfred-prufrock

Farmelo, G. (2013). *Churchill's Bomb*. New York: Basic Books.

Frisch, R. and Peierls, O. (1940). "The Frisch-Peierls Memorandum." Available at: https://web.stanford.edu/class/history5n/FPmemo.pdf

Girard, R. (1979). *Violence and the Sacred.* Baltimore, MD: Johns Hopkins University Press.

International Campaign to Abolish Nuclear Weapons (ICAN). (n. d.). "Hiroshima and Nagasaki bombings." Available at: https://www.icanw.org/hiroshima_and_nagasaki_bombings#:~:text=By%20the%20end%20of%201945,side%20effects%20from%20the%20radiation

Jung, C.G. (1957/2006). *The Undiscovered Self.* Translated by R. F. C. Hull. Penguin Books.

_____. (1960/1975). *Structure and Dynamics of the Psyche.* In *Collected Works*, vol. 8. Translated by R. F. C. Hull. Princeton, NJ: Princeton University Press.

Jung, C.G. (1964). *Civilization in Transition.* In *Collected Works*, vol. 10. Translated by R. F. C. Hull. Princeton, NJ: Princeton University Press.

_____. (1967/1976). *Symbols of Transformation.* In *Collected Works*, vol. 12. Translated by R. F. C. Hull. Princeton, NJ: Princeton University Press

Jungk, R. (1956). *Brighter than a Thousand Suns: The Story of the Men Who Made the Bomb.* Translated by Victor Gollancz and Rupert Hart-Davis. New York: Harcourt, Brace & World.

Lantero, A. (2018). "How Women Helped Build the Atomic Bomb." Available at: https://www.energy.gov/articles/how-women-helped-build-atomic-bomb

Marlan, S. (2005). *The Black Sun: The Alchemy and Art of Darkness.* College Station, TX: Texas A&M University Press.

Rhodes, R. (1988). *The Making of the Atomic Bomb*. NewYork: Simon & Schuster.

Templeton, P. (2021). "Plutonium and Poetry: Where Trinity and Oppenheimer's Reading Habits Met." Available at: https://discover.lanl.gov/news/0714-oppenheimer-literature/

Paranoia: The Madness that Makes History

By Luigi Zoja

With Leonard Cruz

I have been investigating the problem of collective evil and the shadow in the collective. This investigation goes beyond the clinical topic of individual evil and the shadow to embrace the subject at the historical, moral, and cultural levels. I hope to reveal how paranoia is indeed like the subtitle of my book, truly the madness that makes history. A quick survey of history and current events demonstrates that paranoia is, of course, a mental problem and a disturbance of what is considered normal mental function; however, it is altogether too often a motive force that shapes history.

Let's start from the Jungian perspective that emphasizes paranoia and projection as an inherent and universal feature of psychic functioning. We all have a shadow composed of what we do not accept in ourselves. This is the most instinctive dimension of the psyche, and it is projected onto the world.

Animals have evolved mechanisms of mistrust as a means of self-preservation against predators. Human beings have retained these qualities, we too are animals. In fact, an animal in the wild needs to be suspicious of shadows. Let us imagine a deer that perceives a shadow slowly and stealthily creeping toward it; it will instinctively flee, recognizing that this may be a wolf or other predator about to pounce. A wild rabbit feeding at dawn or dusk is acutely attuned to the shadows cast by the low sunlight as a warning of a predator like a hawk that may be circling above. We too have mechanisms that do not permit us to immediately trust everybody. But, in our modern or postmodern urban mass society, our mechanism of distrust becomes permanently activated and easily aroused for faulty reasons. We live permanently among strangers. We are afraid of everything, and of course events like the terrorist attacks of 9/11 have embedded in our collective psyches the worry that at any moment we may be victims of unspeakable horrors.

Once we accept that the shadow, which is unacceptable, must be gotten rid of and expelled from consciousness, we see how easily the contents of the shadow combine with the absolutely *normal* functions of mistrust and suspicion. Let us be clear that it is the excessive deformation of paranoia that constitutes an illness. When paranoia extends itself as an organizing principle of the psyche and forms the bedrock upon which psychic function unfolds, it has the potential to have impact on many lives.

Within the study of psychopathology, some experts point to the appearance of certain clinical disorders at certain times as evidence of society's shaping influence over patterns of illness. For example, in the early days of psychoanalysis, hysteria was a common affliction. It is rarely seen these days. Some writers have noted that the increased prevalence of eating disorders may be rooted in sociocultural forces that idealize thinness. When parents worry about a daughter struggling with an eating disorder, they may worry that she does not possess a real connection to food or that she has idealized thinness to such an extreme that she puts her health and her life in danger. While this is a terrible problem that endangers her, she is not a danger to society. Her mental condition is not contagious.

My use of the adjective "collective" is important because we are linked to history and society at large. Our pathologies are linked. This is a very Jungian approach.

Suppose somebody cultivates the delusion that a certain sector of the population, let's say, for instance, immigrants or Jewish people, are plotting and conspiring against their way of life. Suppose they write books or produce a podcast that becomes popular. Such diatribes can ignite a mass movement. Actually, this person existed; his name was Adolf Hitler. Collective scapegoating, splitting, and projection of the shadow has the potential of being very infectious. In today's climate, paranoid fears of certain groups like immigrants fuel baseless accusations of terrorism or drug dealing. These sorts of eruptions carry with them the risk of repeating the sort of events that Hitler unleashed.

The Diagnostic and Statistical Manual-5 (DSM-5) describes seven features of the paranoid personality disorder. They believe others are 1) using, lying to, or harming them, without apparent evidence thereof; 2) they will have doubts about the loyalty and trustworthiness of others; 3) they fear their confidence will be betrayed; 4) they interpret ambiguous or benign remarks as hurtful or threatening; 5) they hold grudges, without evidence; 6) they believe their reputation or character are being assailed by others and will retaliate; 7) they will be jealous and suspicious without cause of intimate partners. There is ample evidence to support that Hitler met most of these criteria. As to whether he was subject to this last feature, we know too little. We might say he was married to the nationalistic movement.

According to the DSM-5, if a person displays four of the seven criteria, he or she is in the realm of paranoia; however, it only addresses these features as they manifest in the form of individual illness. If a delusion is shared by a group or by the surrounding culture, this does not mean that it ceases to be a pathology, nor does it mean that we should remain unconcerned. To a certain degree, the excessively individualistic assumptions and values embedded in Western psychiatry offer little insight into paranoia that afflicts people at the collective level.

Certain charismatic individuals like Hitler have succeeded in spreading their personal paranoid pathology to others and were able to instigate mass movements. To suggest that simply because large numbers of other people who resonated and agreed with their paranoia make their paranoia normal is to deny a collective phenomenon that history clearly acknowledges.

Such a proposition that the mass embrace of a leader's paranoia makes it normal is quite dangerous politically and eventually militarily. I was living in New York on September 11, 2001, and the day after the terrorist attacks, Murray Stein said to me in a phone conversation, "Luigi, welcome to the United States." That experience of being in New York in the aftermath of 9/11 led me to investigate paranoia more seriously.

It was not the presence of terrorists that aroused my interest. The beliefs and ideas espoused by Osama bin Laden were readily available on the internet and all too familiar. What I recognized was that terrorists and their victims were subject to paranoia. Almost immediately after the 9/11 attacks, people were distrusting of anyone of Middle Eastern descent or anyone who even looked Middle Eastern.

As an immigrant, the day after 9/11 provoked deep sadness in me. Not just the events of September 11, but to witness mass paranoia unleashed and to see the media exploit this was profoundly disturbing. Instead of thoughtful, investigative journalism, many people were exposed through media outlets to various forms of paranoia. Soon paranoia infused American foreign policy so that with blinding speed war was declared on terror, and this further stoked splitting and projection on the collective, cultural level. Over the next 10 years, I devoted myself to investigating collective paranoia and gathered historical material pertaining to paranoia.

On the cover of the Italian edition of my book *Paranoia: follia che fa la storia* (*Paranoia: The Madness That Makes History*) is a photo that appeared on the cover of Life magazine on May 22, 1944, with the following caption: "An Arizona worker writes to her Navy boyfriend a thank-you note for Jap skull he sent her." The shocking thing about this photo is how it testifies to how dehumanized the Japanese had become in the eyes of American enlisted men.

Such barbarism is nothing new. In 2014, a national historic site was commissioned to commemorate the Sand Creek massacre in which troops opened fired upon and killed at least 150 Cheyenne women, children, and the elderly. "Before departing, the troops burned the village and mutilated the dead, carrying off body parts as trophies."[1] Although

---

[1] T. Horowitz, "The Horrific Sand Creek Massacre Will Be Forgotten No More," Smithsonian.com. https://www.smithsonianmag.com/history/horrific-sand-creek-massacre-will-be-forgotten-no-more-180953403/

indigenous peoples scalped their enemies, there is growing consensus that this practice may have been introduced and most certainly increased among indigenous peoples of North America after the arrival of European settlers. The point is that this collective paranoia that relies on splitting and projection upon the enemy leads to the forfeiture of your humanity. The other is rendered as an enemy.

In analyzing this, I have made wide use of Elias Canetti's philosophical essay *Masse und Macht* (*Crowd and Politics*), wherein he speaks of the first dead. Tyrants and unfortunately often also democratic regimes push until we reach the first dead in a confrontation, and then things carry on with a force of their own. Even if only a minority of the population want war, when a critical mass is achieved, historical events are set in motion that may be irreversible. Benito Mussolini was initially part of a minority group when Italy entered World War I. He later increased his power, became dictator, and orchestrated Italy's entry into the Axis alliance during World War II. Once a bloodbath starts, there may be no turning back.

Now, let me sum up some characteristic of the paranoid personality, which once again is something we all have within ourselves. In Jungian terms, the paranoid complex can take over and supplant the ego. When this occurs, the paranoid complex assumes the leading function in the whole personality. In the 18th century when attempts to classify mental disorders was in its infancy, French psychiatry referred to paranoia as *la folie lucide*, the lucid folly. Paranoia may be predicated upon flawed first assumptions, but thereafter its later elaboration and development appear internally logical.

The basic assumption that forms the starting point can be an entirely unproven and absurd idea like the notion that Jewish people were engaged in a vast conspiracy to take over Germany and the entire world. Subsequent assertions often flourish, since they seem to follow logically from the faulty assumptions. For instance, Hitler argued that the Versailles Treaty of 1919 was unjust. This claim was sufficiently true, and it had wide appeal. Even the great 20th-century economist John Maynard Keyes proposed that this treaty would inevitably lead to a new confrontation that would lead to inevitable future conflicts. Before the conference in Versailles, he had proposed no reparations be asked of Germany. Hitler seized upon the unjust terms of the treaty, an idea which was not new. He then forged this nidus of paranoia, which found kinship with the paranoid suspicious nucleus in our personality, with the widespread suffering brought on by hyperinflation within the German economy and unleashed its archetypal potential. A paranoid idea that appears at the collective, cultural level can activate and inflate our archetypal potential. Suddenly, something that had remained hidden in the shadows is fully illuminated and can take on the quality of a mass movement.

One of my Italian colleagues, a Jungian analyst and psychiatrist, wrote an excellent essay on the parallels between religious illumination and paranoia. Remember that what today is rendered as a clinically pathological syndrome in an earlier time may have been interpreted as a religious phenomenon, an illumination, and therefore as a truth. Actually, in the 11th chapter of *Mein Kampf*, Hitler's only propaganda book, he explained very well how he became a radical anti-Semite. Seeing a Jew who was a religious foreign Jew coming from Eastern Europe and was too foreign for him, he had an illumination. He said he was reading about and trying to understand the anti-Semitic question. His family doctor was a Jew, and so he was not so convinced by normal anti-Semitism. He was convinced by his own illumination. After Hitler's illumination, other passages appear that fully demonstrate the hardening of his ideas. Hitler described the process the way some psychiatric textbooks and my Italian colleague did: the forming of granite. Granite is the most solid stone. Hitler calls his ideas about the Jew the granitic foundation of his doctrines; once established, his ideas became as immutable as granite.

After this illumination, Hitler was convinced this would be the basis of all future politics. In the last few moments of his life, he dictated his testament and said: "I've been wrong in the conduct of war. The war is lost. Germany is lost because we have lost the war. But at least I have started the solution of the Jewish problem in Europe, and Europe in general will be thankful."[2] That remained granitic until the very end. This sort of negative projection onto something or some group underscores how limited Western psychiatry with its individualism can be. This is precisely why Jungian psychology with its collective dimension is the best instrument for addressing collective projections.

Even before war was declared, difficult moments became fertile soil for paranoid ideas to take root. In the 1920s, Germany suffered crushing inflation in part as a result of the Treaty of Versailles. The economic hardship produced great insecurity among the German-speaking nations. Inflation ran so rampant that it was not unusual to pay for a meal in advance because the price could go up by the end of the meal

---

[2] A. Hitler, *Mein Kampf*, p. 734.

leaving a customer unable to pay. Such widespread insecurity proved to be a catalyst that allowed a paranoid charismatic leader to rise to power with unprecedented speed.

Paranoia has a specific collective dimension, and it is this collective dimension which interests us as Jungians. We understand that psychoanalysis has shed light on anthropological issues like the very common practice of scapegoating. The psychological underpinnings of scape-goating within the indigenous and tribal societies are often deeply rooted in collective beliefs and social structures. Anthropologically, scapegoating can be understood as a psychological mechanism that helps maintain social cohesion by externalizing negative events, emotions, or perceived threats. This is seen as a collective effort to secure group stability and reinforce cultural norms and identities. The group projects these undesired aspects onto an individual or subgroup, effectively distancing these negative attributes from the society as a whole. This action may provide a collective sense of relief, reaffirming societal boundaries and norms, and reinforcing solidarity among the remaining group members. Scapegoating serves the dual functions of restoring not only each individual's projections, but it also nurtures mutual trust among the members of a tribe because, among other things, the members can cease to project their shadow onto one another.

There is a circularity to the process of paranoia. It's very difficult to extricate oneself from this circularity. I have referred to this feature as the "incline dimension" of paranoia. When we use normal logic, we are able to switch between perspectives in ways that allow a certain degree of self-scrutiny that is absent in paranoia. Normally, there is a lucid part that can question and reassess viewpoints in light of evidence. But paranoia is like being on an incline that naturally leads to a progressive descent. The paranoid individual is radically defensive, and any confrontation that suggests the basic assumptions, arguments, and conclusions are false is met with a granitelike entrenchment and defense. This will often lead to heightened paranoia. This inclined dimension or autotrophic feature allows paranoia to feed upon itself.

Another example from history may help illustrate this phenomenon. In September of 1939, Hitler invaded Poland, which marked the beginning of World War II. By October, Poland had been conquered, and with their meticulous, obsessional mentality, the Nazis made a careful study of the social and economic condition of occupied Poland. They found that the general situation of the population was really bad, but it was made even worse for the Jewish population in October of 1940 when the Jewish residents of Warsaw were ordered to move into the ghetto whose walls were then topped with barbed wire. Ghettos were intended as a temporary step toward what was to become the final solution of exterminating European Jewry. The overcrowding, food shortages, illness, and unsanitary conditions led to a high mortality in the ghettos, and disease and death were rampant.

Ordinarily, one might suppose that seeing the death and disease surging among the ghetto residents would have aroused awareness that these tactics were too harsh. That would be logical. However, Hitler's and Goebbels's reasoning reformulated this, and this intensified the propaganda that Jewish people were dirty, morally corrupt, and a danger, citing the high mortality and disease in the ghettos as confirmatory evidence of the things that had already been projected onto Europe's Jewish population.

Of course, in a dirty population, infections propagate. This situation solidified further the initial prejudice, distortion, and granitic foundations of the "Jewish problem."

I now want to consider Russia and the Soviet Union under Stalin. This was a society in which nearly everything was planned and directed centrally. In a public speech in 1937, Stalin predicted very positive results for economic output, population growth, and per capita income growth. By the end of 1938, the results proved to be quite different from Stalin's public declarations. What happened leading up to that 1937 speech came to be known as the Great Purge in which anyone suspected of having been a supporter of Leon Trotsky and his push for global socialism was eliminated. Stalin imposed what became official state policy of "socialism for one country," in which the focus would no longer be primarily the fomenting of world revolution in accord with classic Marxist-Leninist ideals, but rather to transform the Soviet Union into a socialist state. Stalin's paranoia about the continued presence of Trotskyites throughout the Communist Party led to the Great Purge. What began as a purge of political rivals, quickly expanded to include minorities like the Volga Germans.

Earlier in that decade, Stalin's insistence that Ukrainian farmers be collectivized resulted in a famine that resulted in the death of at least 5 million people, nearly 4 million of whom were Ukrainians. Stalin persecuted intellectuals and rich peasants in his endeavor to extinguish the very idea of Ukraine as a separate nation state with its own identity. In *Red Famine: Stalin's War on Ukraine,* Anne Applebaum writes:

> The Soviet Union's disastrous decision to force peasants to give up their land and join collective

farms; the eviction of "kulaks," the wealthier peasants, from their homes; the chaos that followed—all ultimately the responsibility of Joseph Stalin, the General Secretary of the Soviet Communist Party.[3]

Official records do not reflect the massive population loss nor its economic impact. In fact, when the official statisticians reported the very real losses among the population, they were executed and replaced by individuals willing to furnish the necessary disinformation to perpetuate Stalin's paranoia.

Just a few years later, Hitler's 1941 Operation Barbarossa, which was designed to rid the world of Jewish-Bolshevism, ultimately failed, but it fueled further distrust of Ukraine. Decades later Vladimir Putin used this deep collective distrust of Ukraine as a pretext for invading. Insisting there was an urgent need to de-Nazify its neighbor and protect ethnic Russians living in Ukraine, he launched a war that has heavily relied upon the neo-fascist, white supremacist Wagner Group. This underscores how collective paranoia is easily ignited and reignited.

Whereas most severe mental illnesses alienate a person from society and prove to be a hindrance to a successful life, that may not be true with paranoia. A successful paranoid individual, like a clever politician, may exploit their paranoid personal dimension and arouse similar paranoia among others and thereby enhance their own social position. There is surprisingly little written about the successful paranoid individual. A cunning political leader, particularly one who

---

[3] A. Applebaum-Sikorska, "Preface," *Red Famine: Stalin's War on Ukraine.*

emerges during difficult and conflicted times like during war or the lead-up to war, may find it easier to present his or her paranoid ideas as the only solution to large societal problems. Wartime is a particularly fertile environment for paranoid ideas to flourish since the official doctrine of a warring state often envisions that only total destruction and annihilation of the enemy will suffice. Active warfare does not easily lend itself to seeking negotiated settlements of disputes, nor does it foster an interest in reconciling opposing views, as we might strive for from a Jungian approach. Instead, war tends to deepen the split between parties and further polarize the opposites.

The paranoid leader may turn out to be a highly functioning individual in many respects. However, paranoia feeds upon itself. Once the paranoia emerges, information that might controvert or undermine the paranoia is either rejected or refashioned in ways that serve the paranoid leader's purposes. Paranoid leaders appear to many to be normal, highly capable people. We must remember that, on the one hand, they truly believe there are enemies conspiring against them, while on the other hand, it often seems obvious to others that their paranoia may have been invented to serve politically advantageous positions.

When my book came out in Italy, I was invited to appear on a television program for the book's promotion and was promised that we would not discuss politics except as it reflected psychoanalytically relevant things. The host was intensely opposed to Berlusconi. He showed a video of a speech by Berlusconi in which he claimed there was a conspiracy of leftist judges who were intent on discrediting him. This was the final season of Berlusconi's power. Despite his promise to refrain from inquiring about political topics, the host asked me what I thought and if I thought this was an example of a paranoid person. What could I say?

First, I explained that it is important to evaluate an individual in person before making a diagnosis. However, as a private citizen, I could offer a hypothesis that there were likely two sides to this drama. One side involved the political leader who might be convinced that there was a conspiracy assembled against him since politicians do have enemies. At the same time, he may have exploited the idea that there was a conspiracy against him as a means of increasing his popularity.

As a European, what little I know about the Spanish-American War of 1898 is that it was fueled by two warring newspaper empires owned by William Randolph Hearst and Joseph Pulitzer. In pursuit of higher circulation, their respective New York newspapers engaged in irresponsible reporting, which came to be known as Yellow Journalism. After the sinking of an American ship, the Maine, the Hearst-owned newspapers blamed the Spanish without any substantiating evidence. Pulitzer followed suit, and before long, the drums of war were beating furiously. In many ways, the paranoia that was aroused by the irresponsible journalism, and not the President or the Congress, effectively declared war on Spain. The projection of the shadow onto Spain was an essential factor in shaping that moment in history.

We might divide history broadly into two epochs: the predemocratic period that the French refer to as the *ancient régime* or ancient regime; and the postdemocratic period. The ancient regime involved unelected leaders like kings and tyrants. The political exploitation of paranoia was less frequent then because the leaders did not have to justify their actions. The king was anointed by God to rule on earth, and his visage was often emblazoned on the coin of the realm.

The appearance of democracies permits the expression of different and differing points of view. However, for leaders to secure election or reelection, they often need something to justify to the people that they should be entitled to rule. In their quest for popular support, it may be very tempting to activate paranoid elements.

The political regime often maintains a certain relationship with the use of paranoia that can also be healthy because in thriving democracies, false political assertions can be exposed safely. Yet, leaders can still use paranoia to advance false assertions and spark mass acceptance. Advancing means of communication can accelerate and intensify the effectiveness of a leader seeking to exploit the paranoid element. Since the introduction of the Gutenberg press, the ability to propagandize has reached beyond mere verbal communication to include the printed word. Mass media and more recently social media have become powerful tools in the hands of leaders seeking to use the paranoid elements to their own political advantage. They appeal to a broader audience.

By simplifying and oversimplifying ideas, the media can evoke powerful collective paranoia. Among the most effective simplifications we encounter is the projecting of shadow onto an enemy. In the first phase of this process, the media attribute blame to an *other*. Not that long ago, print media were the primary vehicle, but lately social media can level accusations and blame against an enemy in ways that can spread virally and take on the stature of truth almost instantaneously.

Paranoid leaders often cripple themselves. Consider Joseph Stalin, who appears to have had a paranoid intuition about his statistical commission composed of university professors and highly educated bureaucrats. When Stalin became convinced that the members of the Statistical Commission were seeking to discredit his claims and ruin the image of the lie he had fashioned about the thriving prewar economy and the related growth of the Soviet economy, he simply replaced the members of the Commission with people whose fealty to his paranoia was unquestioned. This new Statistical Commission provided him the data he wanted.

There is a zone of overlap between the paranoid leader and the "normal" person who has an inherent capacity for paranoid thinking. Because we cannot know the mind of another fully, we may not be able to determine to what extent paranoid leaders truly believe the false assertions they promote or if they are instead consciously exploiting the paranoia in the general population. However, once the paranoia is kindled, it tends to feed upon itself.

With the benefit of time, some events declare themselves more clearly as the products of shadow projection or paranoia. In 1976, under the direction of a U.S. Navy Admiral, the sunken U.S.S. Maine was explored, and it seemed to confirm that the Spanish were not responsible for the ship's sinking. But in 1898, the loss of the U.S.S. Maine caused tensions to mount, and the added pressure brought about by the competing newspapers' irresponsible reporting helped fuel paranoia and created the circumstances that became ripe for the paranoia to become a collective infection. We should not ignore that Theodore Roosevelt had a flare for publicity, and through his writing about the taking of San Juan Hill, he secured for himself a celebrated status rivaled only by Admiral George Dewey. Following the assassination of President William McKinley, Roosevelt became President on September 24, 1901.

Looking back at the propaganda disseminated over the Italian radio, we can see that Benito Mussolini was really an originator of the use of radio to sway the masses. Hitler and Stalin quickly followed and found radio to be an enormously effective tool for spreading falsehoods. After World War II, as television was introduced as a state-supported phenomenon, it quickly exploded onto the scene. It should not surprise anyone that Prime Minister Berlusconi, a media tycoon whose family held a majority interest in the largest commercial broadcaster in Italy (Mediaset), would be adept at using every screen he had at his disposal.

Although the Cold War was marked by suspicion and distrust, there was less apparent paranoia, perhaps in part because democracy held it in abeyance. For the most part in the Western world, we did not see rampant military censorship and had formal democracies and a mostly free press, and this served to limit the outbreaks of collective, infectious paranoia.

New dangers have appeared with the growth of media conglomerates like Bertlesmann, Time Warner, Disney, and News Corporation. Rupert Murdoch's vast empire spans broadcasters, major newspapers like the Times of London, Boston Herald, Chicago Sun Times, the New York Post, The Wall Street Journal, and even News Outdoor Russia, and he has had a growing influence upon public perceptions that reached a worrisome apogee in the U.S. with the storming of the United States Capitol on January 6, 2021.

One common theme among the paranoid that is likely absent among Jungians is they are not prone to critical introspection and are unlikely to go in search of their shadow. The paranoid already knows what is wrong, and it is always located outside of them. This is precisely where the Jungian dimension has so much to offer.

It is our Jungian perspective on the collective unconscious, and more precisely the shadow, that may help the world be a little less paranoid and in a manner of speaking become inoculated against collective, infectious paranoia. Even archetypal images like the wolf and the lamb offer us deeper insights into the psychological underpinnings of collective madness. As we see in fairy tales, the wolf wants to find a logical reason to swallow up the lamb, and one way or another, he will find it. In fact, he will project onto the lamb the shadow in order to justify his ravenous and rapacious nature. This is surprisingly similar to the political atmosphere that is currently at play, particularly now that political discourse is so poisoned with mistrust that there appear to be enemies lurking behind every corner.

When I hear citizens of the European Union talking about how we have taken in too many immigrants, a sort of code-switch for the paranoid idea that immigrants are terrorists, I grow concerned. There are many extreme rightwing movements flourishing within the E.U., and talk of fortifying borders or building walls has a great potential for fueling paranoia.

History reminds us that this sort of isolationism has been fraught with failure and can too easily provide the kindling to ignite a conflagration that twice engulfed the European continent during the 20th century. Talk of borders, walls, unwanted immigrants is sustained by the sort of paranoid undercurrent that led to the death of 15 million to 20 million in World War I and another 50 million in World War II. While terrorist attacks have killed hundreds of people, maybe even thousands, it is the collective paranoia that has been responsible for the deaths of millions in the previous century.

There is an intense fascination with the political process in the United States. The media's interest in particular personalities like Donald Trump and Hilary Clinton not only reports on such public figures but also increases their popularity. Traditional news outlets have been vexed by Trump's preternatural ability to capitalize on news even when the substance of a story might have disqualified many other candidates. It seems the governing function provided by the press is disintegrating, and its role is becoming more entertainment and less a guardrail. In many ways, I admire American democracy for its ability often to provide a cleaner and more objective field of discussion in general. That is not to say that America never produces politicians who act like wild beasts. However, let us return to September 12, 2001, when the world felt a collective sympathy and empathy for America. In my opinion, President George W. Bush did not have a true foreign policy, nor was he a well-travelled individual with a large storehouse of experience. In fact, he showed little interest in other countries, so for President Bush, a war on terrorism provided a very simplistic view of geopolitics. Declare war on the bad guys.

We are left with the question of what is available in our culture to counter these unwanted aspects of the media.

Let us begin by recognizing that the direction of this change in media, the press, and the way we are now consuming information easily lends itself to shadow projection. Now more than ever, it is important to distinguish between good and bad media. I rarely watch television, yet I recently attended a televised broadcast of a discussion on terrorism that was informative and largely free of shadow projection onto the other.

I believe there are reputable news organizations that deserve our financial support and deserve to be read, viewed, and shared more than other news outlets. For me, *The New York Times International* is such a news outlet. We can also seek out political and public figures who are relevant and less prone to issuing paranoid messages. In many instances, we see that grassroots activities serve as a sort of antidote to the paranoia and madness that so easily finds expression in modern media.

One figure who comes to mind as an exemplar of the antiparanoid posture is the Argentinian-born conductor Daniel Barenboim. His sublime and delicate skill as a conductor is accentuated when I have witnessed him conducting an orchestra of young Palestinian and Israeli musicians. In these concerts, we see on full display that music is a shared language, and shadow projection is conspicuously absent. Imagine if media chose to amplify such examples, and we as consumers of media saw fit to throw our support behind such figures. When their examples have the opportunity to compete with the intensely alluring and charismatic figures who engage in paranoid shadow projection, there is something kindled in the human spirit that can counter the unwanted effects.

During the televised roundtable discussion on terrorism and a united or disunited Europe, data from the Pugh Research Center was cited in which certain countries like Poland and Hungary perceive the percentage of the population that are Muslims to be 50 to 70 times higher than their actual representation in the general population. Such distorted perceptions are impressive, and they inform us of the powerful presence of our shadow and what we perceive even when there is little evidence to support it. For example, among Hungarians surveyed the estimate was 7 percent when in fact only 0.1 percent of the population identified as Muslim. Some countries like Germany seemed to distort the percentages less (19 percent when the actual percentage is 6), the perception in many Eastern European countries was more exaggerated, perhaps a result of old repressed nationalism during a half century of communist rule. What these data reveal is that what is perceived arises from the shadow more than the reality that surrounds us.

No country is immune. To some extent, the German experience of the rise of Nazism inoculated many of the German people against extreme shadow projections, yet there still exist extreme right-wing groups espousing paranoid beliefs. For example, PEGIDA (Patriotische Europäer gegen die Islamisierung des Abendlandes) is an extreme right-wing movement centered in East Germany where there are many fewer Muslims than in West Germany. One of the 19 position statements from 2015 document states the group is for the "preservation and protection of our Judeo-Christian, Western culture."

One can say that a country or society has its own narrative, and sometimes the narratives of neighboring countries are like mirror images of one another. Consider the strikingly different narratives circulating among Russian and Ukrainian citizens. Murray Stein recounted to me a story of a Russian student at ISAPZURICH who explained that to a large degree Vladimir Putin is not simply deceiving the Russian people, but he is a representative of the collective Russian paranoia that exists in the Russian people.

With the fall of the Soviet Union, Russia found itself in a vulnerable, insecure state much as Germany did following World War I. This provided a rich soil for paranoia to take root. The Soviet Union suffered a radical defeat, and although it was not a military defeat, it proved to be a political and economic one. This may well have made the people more prone to embrace the history-making collective madness we are witnessing being played out in the trenches of Ukraine.

Adolf Hitler's rise to power was facilitated by the vulnerability, insecurity, and hardships that were visited upon Germany after World War 1. Hitler didn't have to convince the people of a paranoid view of the Jews; he just had to elicit the paranoia that already existed and then focus the German will upon the need to fend off the perceived threat whose flames he stoked. The same thing is happening today as paranoid perceptions are stoked by politicians and the media. It is very hard to break free of a collective paranoia, and it turns out to be surprisingly easy to exploit the collective perception of a threat from an enemy out there. Playing on the message of Navy Commandant Oliver Perry to General Harrison after a victory during the war of 1812— "We have met the enemy, and they are ours"—Walt Kelly has the cartoon figure Pogo speak a more psychological truth in the 1960s about the Vietnam war: "We have met the enemy, and they are us."[4]

This collective madness that shapes history is taking place on both sides of political divides. Undoubtedly, as the West considers Russia's aggression against Ukraine there, there exists a substantial degree of shadow projection

---

4   https://www.dictionary.com/browse/we-have-met-the-enemy--and-they-are-us

that is amplified by the media and politicians seeking to exploit the vulnerabilities perceived by people in Western democratic countries. We must remember that as Jungians, we are faithful adherents to complex psychology; it does not serve us to engage in simplification and projection. As I have written elsewhere, many geopolitical conflicts and situations can be solved without resorting to paranoia, even when those who oppose us engage in such paranoia. This tendency to paranoia is a recurring theme when we consider examples like the conflicts between Israel and its surrounding Arab neighbors or Catalonia and the government of Spain.

Occasionally, we encounter examples of how differences can be resolved without resorting to paranoia. In Czechoslovakia, the people acknowledged that some were Czech while others were Slovak, and without spilling a drop of blood and without fists in the eye, the people embraced a common enough identity that did not descend into collective madness. This is a particularly striking example, because Czechoslovakia was a hotbed of conflict during the Cold War years.

There are examples within professional societies, too, where referendums can lead to further splitting, disunion, and projection of shadow. Under such circumstances where a faction of a society wishes to split away, it is sometimes best to allow the split to occur politely and with as little animosity as possible. The conflicts may end there. I am referring here to events that took place with the formation of the International School of Analytical Psychology in Switzerland. In these cases, there is nothing worse than a forced marriage.

Observing the contemporary state of U.S. politics from an international perspective, particularly the rise of figures like Donald Trump and the implications of terrorism, one could see how this could potentially induce feelings of paranoia.[5] However, this subject demands a deeper level of contemplation given its complex nuances.

Adopting a more clinical perspective, the way a Jungian analyst might approach a paranoid client provides useful guidance and context. Such a scenario is not commonplace due to the inherent suspicion and reticence of individuals suffering from paranoia. In a one-to-one consultation, navigating paranoia poses a significant challenge.[6] Analysts' interpretations often become enmeshed in the patient's paranoia, fostering distrust and further dissuading help-seeking. This reflects that feature of paranoia that feeds on itself.

In long-term analysis, a paranoid phase is possible to remain engaged with and eventually move beyond. A paranoid phase in analysis often manifests in individuals who have nursed high ambitions but failed to achieve success. Struggling to comprehend their failure, these individuals may succumb to conspiracy theories, attributing their lack of progress to external malice stemming from jealousy of their perceived abilities—a perspective often intertwined with elements of megalomania.[7] Over time, such paranoia may subside as specific tensions and projections dissipate—for instance, following a divorce.

Historical figures like Hitler and Stalin have often been scrutinized through the psychiatric lens. A prevailing conclusion posits that they exhibited traits of narcissistic

---

5 See L. Greenfeld, *Mind, Modernity, Madness*.
6 See L. Zoja, "Violence in History, Culture, and the Psyche."
7 Ibid.

personality disorder and paranoia.[8] These characteristics have distinct features, but they can coexist in a person like those who may identify with more than one religion. Psychological disturbances can manifest concurrently. Moreover, the individual swept up in a group acquires, as Freud says, a sense of invincible power and will be less prone to check himself.[9]

Psychiatry, historiography, and psychoanalysis converge to typify Stalin as predominantly paranoid, supported by the analysis of historical evidence.[10] In contrast, Hitler was not only paranoid but also manic-depressive. However, addressing their heinous acts of mass murder raises further questions: Were they also psychopathic?

Responding to this inquiry reveals a significant overlap of pathologies. The underlying amorality is a key determinant. Psychopaths typically exhibit indifference toward moral issues, whereas figures like Hitler and Stalin were deeply entangled with the concept of evil, a characteristic commonly linked to paranoia.[11] They externalized evil, viewing it as a component of the "other," and believed their actions could eradicate it.

However, they did not display classic psychopathic tendencies such as wealth accumulation. Instead, they dedicated themselves to their respective missions. This observation prompts further inquiry: Could a leader less paranoid but more corrupt be less destructive? The discernment becomes complex when leaders exploit pervasive national paranoia to consolidate power. Former

---

[8] See N. Ghaemi, *A First -Rate Madness*.
[9] S. Freud, *Group Psychology and the Analysis of the Ego*.
[10] See. N. Ghaemi, *A First-Rate Madness*.
[11] See R.D. Hare, *Without Conscience*.

Italian Prime Minister Berlusconi provides a pertinent example of this dynamic. Distinguishing genuine belief from the exploitation of paranoia for personal gain can prove challenging and may only become apparent retrospectively, as historians unravel the intricacies of such leadership.[12]

Leaders like Hitler and Stalin exhibited a steadfast conviction in their beliefs—a defining feature of a paranoid personality. They were true believers—Stalin in Marxism-Leninism and Hitler in anti-Semitism—unlike leaders such as Trump, who display traits of narcissism and unpredictability rather than an unwavering, foundational belief.[13] In the run up to the 2016 U.S. Presidential Election, various contributors explored narcissism in the contemporary context.[14]

The rise of modern terrorism has fueled national and international paranoia. The perception and projection of terrorism onto Muslim immigrants exemplify this phenomenon. However, while terrorism is a legitimate threat, it may not pose the most significant danger to humanity. One such overshadowed threat is climate change, which despite its potentially catastrophic implications, often fails to receive due attention. High-profile terror attacks, such as those in Brussels, occupy substantial media space, whereas discussions around climate change and its long-term ramifications are frequently sidelined.

Unlike terrorism, which presents a clear adversary, climate change implicates us all—we contribute to the crisis through our excessive consumption and lifestyle habits. It

---

[12] See D. Albertazzi, et. al., "Di lotta e di governo: The Lega Nord and Rifondazione Comunista in office."
[13] See J.M. Post, *Narcissism and Politics*.
[14] See L. Cruz, et. al., *A Clear and Present Danger: Narcissism in the Era of Donald Trump*.

is easier to confront a known, immediate enemy than to acknowledge a diffuse, slow-moving threat wherein we are all complicit. Consequently, despite the potential for significant impact, we often downplay or ignore the risks posed by climate change. Thus, our collective response to these threats exposes not only our capacity for paranoia but also our propensity to sidestep responsibility when the enemy is elusive, and the blame rests with us.

References

Albertazzi, D., McDonnell, D., & Newell, J. L. (2009). "Di lotta e di governo: The Lega Nord and Rifondazione Comunista in office." *Party Politics*, 15(3), 315-336.

Applebaum-Sikorska, A. (2018). "Preface." *Red Famine: Stalin's War on Ukraine*. New York: Penguin Books.

Arendt, H. (1963). *Eichmann in Jerusalem: A Report on the Banality of Evil*. New York: Viking Press.

Cruz, L., Buser, S. (2016). *A Clear and Present Danger: Narcissism in the Era of Donald Trump*. Asheville, NC: Chiron Publications.

Freud, S. (1989). *Group Psychology and the Analysis of the Ego*. New York: W.W. Norton.

Gardiner, S. M. (2011). *A Perfect Moral Storm: The Ethical Tragedy of Climate Change*. Oxford: Oxford University Press.

Ghaemi, N. (2011). *A First-Rate Madness: Uncovering the Links Between Leadership and Mental Illness*. New York: Penguin Books.

Gifford, R. (2011). "The Dragons of Inaction: Psychological Barriers that Limit Climate Change Mitigation and Adaptation." *American Psychologist*, 66(4), 290–302.

Greenfeld, L. (2013). *Mind, Modernity, Madness: The Impact of Culture on Human Experience*. Cambridge, MA: Harvard University Press.

Hare, R. D. (1999). *Without Conscience: The Disturbing World of the Psychopaths Among Us*. New York: Guilford Press.

Hitler, A. (2016). *Mein Kampf,* Eine kritische Edition. Munich & Berlin Institut für Zeitgescchichte.

Horowitz, T. (2014). "The Horrific Sand Creek Massacre Will Be Forgotten No More." Smithsonian.com. https://www.smithsonianmag.com/history/horrific-sand-creek-massacre-will-be-forgotten-no-more-180953403/

Pape, R. (2005). *Dying to Win: The Strategic Logic of Suicide Terrorism*. New York: Random House.

Post, J. M. (2014). *Narcissism and Politics: Dreams of Glory*. Cambridge: Cambridge University Press.

Zoja, L. (2009). *Violence in History, Culture, and the Psyche. Essays*. New Orleans, LA: Spring Journal Books.

_____. (2011). *Paranoia: La Follia Che FA la storia*. Milan, Italy: Bollati Boringhieri.

_____. (2017). *Paranoia: The Madness That Makes History*. London: Routledge.

The Shadow and the Search for a New Ethic: A Dialogue

Henry Abramovitch with Murray Stein

Murray Stein: The idea of the shadow is deeply woven into Jung's psychological theory, and the problem of evil occupied his mind profoundly, especially after the Second World War and during the last 20 years of his life. Erich Neumann also took up this topic profoundly. The focus here will be on what we've called "the responsible self." This brings a dynamic view because we want to think about what we as human beings, who are so subject to these shadow forces and temptations, can conduct ourselves as moral and ethical beings in the face of our ignorance and our proclivities to project the shadow and gang up on others who carry these projections. How can we confront the problem of the shadow and the problem of evil responsibly? Henry Abramovitch, an Israeli analyst, will elaborate his approach, ideas, and perspectives.

Henry Abramovitch: I'd like to begin with Erich Neumann's famous book, *Depth Psychology and a New Ethic*. There he focuses his attention on the problem of evil and a new ethic.

Murray Stein: This was a very controversial book when it first appeared. In Zurich, it was not received with much favor by Jungians at first. Over time and with the approval of Jung himself, it has become a classic in the Jungian literature. Henry, why don't you begin by sketching in some of Erich Neumann's main ideas in this book.

Henry Abramovitch: I feel privileged to present the work of Erich Neumann because he first brought the Jungian psychology to Israel, established Israel Association of Analytical Psychology (one of the founding members of IAAP), and is the founding ancestor of our institute, Israel Institute of Jungian Psychology in honor of Erich Neumann. His inspiration for confronting evil came directly from what was being done in Europe in his time. But it was also inspired by kind of an active imagination that he went through that he described in his correspondence with Jung, as I will describe later.

Neumann felt that we could think about ethical aware- ness in three stages and each with a distinctive view of evil. Each also required a distinctive therapeutic response. The first stage he called the stage of primal unity, and it was based emotionally on the primal unity of the mother and infant. This is a stage when people feel a tremendous loyalty to people in their group with an intense sense of solidarity and belonging. Primal unity provides that profound human need for belonging, meaning, and of togetherness. It can be benign, as in profound identification with your football team. From the moral point of view, any attack on one of the members is always an attack on all. Right and wrong are not based upon a philosophical or intellectual concern about the nature of the deed but rather on the profound belief that loyalty to the group is good, while disloyalty is bad. Evil is perceived as coming from a person outside the group who is challenging or attacking the group and thus threatening to undermine its primal unity.

Primal unity operates differently from a modern legal system in which individuals are held accountable for their proven misdeeds. If I assault you, I should be punished and nobody else. But in the stage of primal unity, anyone in the murderer's group can be punished, because responsibility is a group responsibility and not an individual one. I live in a part of the world where such primal unity dynamics are very much a daily reality. For instance, if a member of an extended family of Bedouins sheds blood, there is a moral commandment that someone from the wounded family kill somebody in the other person's extended family. It's not about right and wrong on an individual level. Issues of right and wrong are dealt with on a collective level.

Sporting events bring out the group identity of primal unity. Traditionally, one hates the fans of the other team just because they are the Other. Sometimes, if things get out of control, you might actually become violent toward them. But consider how easily one feels that it's good to hate a whole group of people who have done nothing bad to you except to be other. I think this might explain why Neumann's book was accepted so badly by Jung's Swiss disciples when it was first published. It was not because of the book's contents, but because he was an outsider to the Zurich insiders and his view was threatening to the primal unity of this group that had centered themselves around Jung.

Murray Stein: What about strong feelings of nationalism? These are so present throughout the world today.

Henry Abramovitch: Yes, but nationalism itself goes through various stages. Primal nationalism in the stage of primal unity is sentiment based on "anti." We are unified against some real or imaginary enemy. Anybody who is challenging this primal unity becomes an enemy. In the aftermath of 9/11, the Bush government, I believe, felt ashamed that it had not protected the American people from a terrorist threat. Impulsively, the Bush administration wanted to hit back, to invade Iraq or Pakistan in order to take revenge. Anyone who expressed the need for a bit of further reflection was seen as in league with the enemy. The Congress actually changed the word for French fries to Freedom fries because the French people were not 100% behind these retaliations. But nationalism doesn't always have that much intensity and exclusiveness. It can be more nuanced. I have a Danish son-in-law. In Denmark, I have found, people are quite patriotic. They fly their flag at any significant event, even on birthdays. The flag is considered sacred, having dropped from heaven at a crucial point in Danish history. Danes have an intense pride in their flag and their country, but it is patriotism that is not based on excluding the other. It might be called "patriotism without enemies." Canadian nationalism is similar to this. A sense of belonging is a very profound human need, and that's really what Jung spoke about in his phrase "modern man is in search of a soul." The modern person is homeless. Jung meant this as a search for a home, without which a person is existentially alienated in a way that people have not been in the past.

The second stage of moral development is what Neumann called "the old ethic." Such radical development is always made by introverted, intuitive types, those people who are able to hear a New Voice in solitude, often in the desert. They return to teach new ethical ideals and become metaphorically like a self for their community. What they bring amounts to a spiritual revolution. Armed with such a strong vision, these revolutionaries are empowered to stand against a crowd. Buddha's teachings of nonattachment, the Five Pillars of Islam, the Ten Commandments, and so forth, are all based on the ideals of an individual with immense personal self-control.

In the *Sayings of the Fathers,* a foundational Rabbinic document, the question is asked: "Who is a hero?" And the answer is given: "The hero is the person who can restrain his evil urges." This ideology of the old ethic is all about the control of urges and impulses, such as sexuality, aggressiveness, envy, etc. Perfect control will lead to spiritual perfection, it is taught, and then the individual will be completely good. The spiritual founders are usually extraordinary individuals who are able to live and work authentically at this new moral level. Their disciples are imbued with a missionary sense and inspired to spread the Truth, but they are not able to sustain that level of self-control. Neumann argues that all of the biblical heroes violated some of the ethical norms of their native society, and that is an essential part of the ethical awareness process. For example, Abraham abandoned his aging father and was ready to murder his own son. Jacob obtained his father's blessing but only through deceit. Neumann believed the old ethic did serve to strengthen the ego against the shadowy forces of the unconscious and so stimulated the development of individual morality. However, in the old ethic, the inner life is based on repression and suppression, which Neumann saw as sapping the true strength of the personality from its inherent, animalistic, and transcendent abilities. It is similar to Robert Bly's critique of unhealthy masculinity, which he called "soft men" who are sensitive and good feminists but cut off from their own vitality.

The old ethic, inevitably, leads to projecting the shadow elements onto other groups, whether Blacks, Jews, Gypsies, Gays, or others. The more an individual or a society feels threatened, the stronger the urge to annihilate the shadow bearers. The dynamic of the old ethic is very much reflected in the motif of the hostile brothers, which Jung discusses in *Answer to Job*: Cain and Abel, Jacob and Esau, Seth and Osiris, Romulus and Remus. According to Neumann, a genocidal urge is built into the psychology of the old ethic. Or in a different formulation: Trying to be too good leads directly to atrocities.

Murray Stein: Henry, let me just add a point here if I may. I was in Rome recently and took the opportunity to visit Michelangelo's famous statue of Moses in the Basilica San Pietro in Vincoli. Freud, as you know, was in awe of this work of art, and what he says about it in his last book, *Moses and Monotheism,* is that it shows us a man who is successfully restraining his rage. Moses has come down from the mountain with the stone tablets in his arms. They are inscribed with the Commandments by the hand of the Lord. And Moses sees what has happened down below in his absence. The people have created a golden calf and are worshipping it. They have regressed to paganism. Moses is enraged, but he controls his emotion as he gazes at them with the tablets in his arms. Freud looked with great admiration at this image of a great man just at the moment of containing his hot emotion for the sake of something higher, something better. The people, however, could not bear the laws he brought to them from on high, and so they rose up in fury and killed Moses. This is Freud's summary analysis of the human condition. Few can restrain their emotions. Freud was like Moses. As an analyst, he was in control of his emotions, and this provided a model for his patients.

Henry Abramovitch: I entirely agree. The traditional Freudian analyst had to be completely restrained in a way that I think doesn't allow for spontaneity or synchronicity, which are such important aspects of analysis as I see it. It is significant to note that Michelangelo's statue of Moses is based on a misreading of the original Hebrew text. Michelangelo put horns on Moses's head. The Hebrew text in context, however, does not mean "horns" but "rays of light." Moses descended from Mount Sinai, literally glowing.

If we analyze that key passage in the Bible, I believe it is possible to suggests that when Moses came down from the mountain and saw his people worshipping the golden calf, God wanted to kill all the people. At this point, Moses becomes the "*navi*," or prophet, continuing the tradition of Abraham, the first prophet. The Hebrew sense of a *navi* is somebody who restrains the destructive side of God. Later, Moses also chastises the people when they're doing wrong. Thus, the *navi* has this double role, mediating the people to the Divinity and mediating the Divinity to the chosen people.

Moses at the end of his life tried to pass on this tradition, saying, "Here I place before you the good and the bad. Therefore, choose the good." It's a choice all the time. The bad is always there in front of us.

Murray Stein: It's right in line with existentialism, isn't it? It's all about choice. Choose the good.

Henry Abramovitch: The new ethic, as Neumann argues, teaches that evil must be accepted. Evil exists in the world, and evil exists in us. Neumann felt we have an unconscious desire to know evil that is expressed in the fascination with vampire movies and serial killers but also with such figures in Shakespeare's tragedies as Iago and Othello and Lady McBeth.

To further emphasize the point, Neumann drew on Hassidic tradition which argued that acknowledgment of one's own evil is good and that to be too good is evil. Hence, evil done in a conscious way is ethically good. In a way, it is consistent with Jung's key idea of the need to hold the opposites together. Neumann does not give specific examples of the new ethic—I think he understood that it could not be formulaic—but I think civil disobedience, from Antigone to anti-Putin protests, may be examples. Antigone knowingly does "evil" in the eyes of the state because she is obedient to higher ideal and is willing to face consequences of her actions to bury her brother.

Murray Stein: We had the same type of situation in the States when civil rights protesters violated civil law by marching through the streets of Selma, Alabama. Of course, they were arrested and jailed. We see this also today in protests against global warming, people gluing themselves to streets and paintings. It looks crazy, but it is response to a higher call.

Henry Abramovitch: People who saved Jews during the Holocaust were asked why they did it, endangering their families to save someone they barely knew. Their response was amazing. They said they didn't do anything special: Wouldn't anybody do the same? That's how an authentically good person feels about doing the good. It was just the right thing to do. All new ethic actions are without any ego. In contrast, Nazi morality was like Neumann's stage of primal unity. Loyalty to Hitler and loyalty to das Volk were the highest and, indeed, the only value.

Murray Stein: Henry, when you teach about ethics within the context of Jungian groups and training programs, how do you go about it?

Henry Abramovitch: I call it "stimulating ethical awareness." Because ethics and ethical violations derive from the imagination, I always start with an active imagination. I usually ask for starters: "What is the worst thing a therapist can do?" In a vicarious way, it forces therapists to confront the reality of shadow within the therapeutic space. I have asked this question in dozens of countries, and what is amazing is that I inevitably hear new and different answers. In China, people were most concerned about acting out an "authority" transference that patients projected onto them; in Israel, people often speak about abandonment, like inviting a patient for a session and then deliberately not showing up. What is also striking is that many of these "worst" things would not be covered by the codes of ethics.

Therefore, the next topic I focus on is to have participants talk about their group's code of ethics. All Jungian societies in IAAP have ethics codes and codes of practice. But very few members have studied or even read the codes. For these codes of ethics to be effective, these documents need to be part of a living, vital "ethical community" that understands there are difficult issues that need to be addressed by the community as a whole. I therefore advocate regular public readings and study of the codes. The preface of the ethics code of my society, the Israel Institute of Jungian Psychology, tries to encourage analysts to face ethical dilemmas as deeply as possible: "Analysts are regularly caught up in conflict between opposing ethical demands and the best way to deal with conflict is a genuine inner struggle. These guidelines are designed to assist in that effort..."

Public reading and study of codes may go a long way to heighten moral sensitivity and create an ethically cohesive community, which can then stand against shadowy events.

Then, using a Talmudic technique in workshop format, we examine real life clinical dilemmas, which occur in what Primo Levi called a "gray zone." These dilemmas are complex and not given to simple solutions.

WARNING SIGNALS

Ethical violations are typically not impulsive acts but part of a gradual process on an ethically slippery slope. Research has revealed that there are clear warning signals that we are sliding. In connection with sex with a patient, the warning signs include giving special favors and longer sessions, especially if it is the last session of the day. However, in general, the most important and reliable warning signal for any ethical issue is secrecy, doing something you would not want to become known by your colleagues. "Is this what a therapist/analyst does?" is a question we must be continually asking ourselves as we approach the gray zone. If we hesitate, even momentarily, we are at risk and should immediately consult with a colleague and ethics committee since "no one should have to deal with such troubling ethical dilemmas alone."[1] The cover-up, as we know from King David to Watergate, is often worse than the original

---

[1] P.A. Dewald and R.W. Clark, *Ethics Case Book of the American Psychoanalytic Association,* p. 49.

misdeed. Facing up to it is the first step of returning and perhaps forgiveness.

KEY CASES

The main way to explore the gray zones and strengthen our ethical muscles is by intense analysis of key cases, examined in what I call a Talmudic manner. The Talmudic approach is in some ways the opposite of the code approach. Codes of Ethics describe general abstract principles and ideal modes of behavior and procedures. The Talmudic method uses specific examples to build up general principles, which are then challenged by further examples that push the conceptual boundaries as far as possible. Inquiry is grounded in examples and questions, rather than abstractions.[2] The goal is to think through all the conceptual implications of the case and have ethical muscles primed for an unexpected eventuality.

Here is a case which I will call, "Warning a colleague." A colleague, Jacob, comes to you and says that he has just received a diagnosis of colon cancer with an uncertain prognosis. Jacob has a full practice, including analysands, candidates in analysis and in supervision. Jacob is receiving chemotherapy and feels well enough to continue working. He feels, in fact, that the illness has made him a better analyst by allowing him to better understand patients' experiences. But Jacob is not sure what to do. He has come to you for advice.

This case forces us to consider something none of us want to face. Good clinical practice requires that patients of seriously ill or dying analysts be transferred ahead of time. Sadly, I know from personal experience with dying

---

[2] See A. Steinsaltz, *The Essential Talmud.*

colleagues how difficult it was for them to let go of their patients who provided them with so much vitality and meaning.[3] Each died while still seeing patients. The sudden death of an analyst has a profound and lasting effect on analysands. Most are unable to mourn a beloved analyst who abandoned them without time to say goodbye. Many patients, therefore, are unable to attach to a new analyst and chronically fear further abandonment. My dying colleagues were too focused on their own need to be needed and so unable to foresee the impact of their impending demise on their patients. A dying or even seriously ill therapist who does not offer to transfer patients is committing a serious ethical violation.

In the U.K., it is mandatory to deposit an updated patient list with a trusted colleague. That is what I did when I was sick.

WARNING A COLLEAGUE

The case of the seriously ill colleague raises the difficult issue of how and when to warn colleagues when they are crossing beyond the gray zone. It is easiest to do nothing, but in Israel we are very sensitive to what can happen when one remains silent and does not speak up.

Warning a colleague is hard; what is needed is a community culture in which warnings are part of a collective responsibility of the whole community.

In my institute after intensive discussion, we worked out some rules of thumb about how to warn as part of our ethical community:

---

[3] See A.H. Kaplan and D. Rothman, "The dying psychotherapist."

--- if you do **not** warn an analyst in danger, then you are complicit;

--- warnings should be done in pairs, at least one who knows the analyst well;

--- a personalized approach should be worked out in advance for how to warn this person, at this time;

--- encounter done without threats but with an emphasis on caring for the colleague and consequence.

Murray, think of how you would warn a close colleague.

Murray Stein: At our school in Zurich, we have set up a Committee of Care made up of three senior analysts. It is their responsibility to do as you suggest. As you say, it's very difficult. The older analysts who are fading dread a call from the Committee of Care. We have jokes about it. What I would do, Henry, if I thought a colleague was going beyond the gray zone would be to notify the Committee of Care to look into it. It's their task to empathically investigate and confront the individual analyst in question.

Henry Abramovitch: In most societies when there is serious ethical violation, the response follows the stages of Neumann. The first response is to fall back into something like primal unity. An ethical complaint about one member is perceived as an attack on the whole society, and the whistleblower is attacked and scapegoated. The collective urge is to destroy that person and feel good about it. In the response based on the Old Ethic, in contrast, the members feel betrayed by the person against whom the complaint was lodged. The feeling is "we trusted them and they have betrayed us." Archetypally, he or she takes on the role of

Judas and should be kicked out of the society. They take the role of the scapegoat whose sacrifice will renew the group.

In using the New Ethic, the analytical society would not see it exclusively as an individual problem but as something groups must deal with as a conscious and ethically responsible community. Questions must be asked like: How did our society allow this thing to happen? How did our training fail ethically? And why has this event occurred among us? Why has it come now, at this time?

Murray Stein: And is there not the possibility of forgiveness for ethical violations? Instead of excluding the perpetrator, why not use the principle of restorative justice and allow them to return to community?

Henry Abramovitch: Let me contrast fundamental differences between the Jewish view of forgiveness with the nature of Christian forgiveness. In the Christian tradition, forgiveness is conceived of as an internal psychological process that you have to go through. You can and indeed should forgive someone who harmed you or your children "in your heart" even if you have never met the person, even if they never had asked for forgiveness. Not to forgive creates a burden within the soul and psyche of the person, and forgiveness is central to spiritual progress of a Christian. The Jewish view is very different and is essentially interpersonal. If I sinned against you, Murray, I must go and ask forgiveness directly from you, in person. Even then, in the Jewish perspective, you have no religious obligation to forgive me. I cannot force you to forgive me. If I am unforgiven, not even God can forgive! *Yom Kippur,* the holiest day of the Hebrew Year, can only provide reconciliation between the person and the divine. Traditionally, Jews try to seek forgiveness for sins between his/her fellows, separately and in advance.

I will offer a clinical example of how Neumann's perspective helped me deal with a difficult clinical ethical dilemma and ultimately find an unexpected third way illustrating Neumann's New Ethic.

I had this patient who was a highly regarded mental health professional and a very good therapist in her own right. After a full year of working well together, she suddenly revealed to me that in her previous therapy, she had been sexually abused by her therapist. I can tell you my first reaction was in the tradition of the Old Ethic I described above. I became enraged at her previous therapist. I was on the warpath. I was going to report him. I was going to take away his license. I was going to do all sorts of things so I would feel good and he would feel bad! Then, suddenly, I realized I had completely and emotionally abandoned my patient. She said clearly that she did have the strength to consider making a complaint and what she needed now was my support.

We worked on this issue for a long time. Like many women who undergo abuse, she felt it must be somehow her own fault. Moreover, the therapeutic experience with the previous therapist had been mostly positive, and she did not want to lose this feeling. We were able to build a strong therapeutic alliance, and eventually she came up with a third way between reporting the violation and not reporting it. She decided to confront him with what had happened and have him admit that he had done something very wrong and inappropriate. Then she demanded that he never treat any woman ever again in therapy. She threatened him that if he violated this pledge, she would report him to the authorities will all the fury a woman can show. She had held the good and the bad of this experience together. She was an Orthodox Jewish woman, and her approach was based on the Jewish idea that forgiveness can be offered if one truly feels that this offense will never be repeated.

Finally, in workshops, I advocate doing a simulation of an actual ethical complaint.

It is a kind of moral leadership, this confronting of people in a way that turns evil into good without denying the reality of evil. And those are the real heroes of our time.

Murray Stein: Yes, moral geniuses in a way.

Henry Abramovitch: Moral geniuses, that's right.

Murray Stein: I want to go back to Neumann for a moment, Henry. I've heard you mention elsewhere something about what inspired his book on ethics, but I didn't catch the full story.

Henry Abramovitch: Let me tell you what inspired Neumann to write the New Ethics book. It was a dream. He writes:

> I seemed to be commissioned to kill the apeman in the profound primal hole. As I approached him, he was hanging, by night, sleeping on the cross above the abyss, but his-crooked-single eye was staring into the depths of this abyss. While it at first seemed that I was supposed to blind him, I all of a sudden grasped his "innocence," his dependence on the single eye of the Godhead, which was experiencing the depths through him, which was a human eye.

Then, very abridged, I sank down in opposite this single eye, jumped into the abyss, but was caught by the Godhead, which carried me on the "wings of his heart." After that, this single eye opposite the apeman closed and it opened on my forehead.[4]

Murray Stein: Can you explain how this dream led Neumann to write his book *Depth Psychology and the New Ethic*? Did receiving this eye in his forehead mean that he could see a new dimension of moral problems? Is this the ego-self axis that gives a new perspective?

Henry Abramovitch: I understand the dream as inspiration for the New Ethic as follows. The beginning of the dream represents the situation of the Old Ethic, in which the good must destroy the primitive, the bad, and annihilate that consciousness. But when Neumann literally and symbolically approaches the apeman, he experiences him through the archetype of innocent victim, connecting depth and surface as in the transcendence function. Leaping into the abyss but being carried by "wings of the heart" allowed Neumann to hold together the opposites of the primitive and spiritual in a new way. Having the consciousness of the apeman but also at the same time the spiritual link to the heart of the Godhead provided him the psychic inspiration to write *Depth Psychology and the New Ethic*, which links good and evil in a new way.

Morality necessarily includes a cost/benefit kind of calculation, especially when you need to make terrible

---

[4] M. Liebscher (ed.), *Analytical Psychology in Exile*, p. 331.

choices. But morality does have, I think, an absolute sense of the self. And maybe you can call it the responsible self.

Murray Stein: Yes. I like that term. It's the title of a book by a theological mentor of mine, H. Richard Niebuhr.

Henry Abramovitch: Moral acts ... You know, it's just like you're going to do the right thing because it's the right thing to do.

Murray Stein: And speaking of the inferior parts, you could say the moral self, or the ethical self, takes care of them, takes care of the inferior functions also. It doesn't just overvalue the superior functions and neglect the inferior ones or try to destroy them.

Henry Abramovitch: A healthy ego-self axis is an expression of the responsible self.

Murray Stein: Yes, that's a good way to put it.

Henry Abramovitch: Evil occurs when ego is trying to cut itself off from the self, or when ego identifies with self, in what I call "the god complex." This occurs in cults and cult leaders.

Murray Stein: When the ego is cut off from the self, you become a "one-sided" person who sees things in a monochromatic way and absolutizes. But the ego-self axis, on the contrary, creates a balance because the self is made up of polarities.

Henry Abramovitch: And how can I explain this? It's like water for a plant. The self provides nutrients for the ego but is not in them. Like a lotus image in Buddhism, the self has these deep roots, it's muddy, and all the different parts of the unconscious are there.

Murray Stein: I think it's important from Neumann's perspective to take the self into account and not only the ego. Otherwise, you get the Old Ethic all over again.

Henry Abramovitch: To test whether a situation is truly ethical, you have to describe the situation. Then ask, how would you feel if you were A? Then, what if you were B? If you were happy with this situation no matter what, then we can say it's ethical. There are simple techniques you can use with children who often squabble about who gets more. The solution is for one child to cut the cake and the second child to choose first which piece they get.

Murray Stein: That's a good solution. I like that. Also the notion of transparency struck me. You know, there's a lot of talk now about transparent systems and people being transparent. I think what that means is full disclosure of possible conflicts of interest and so on, so that you can put them out there in the open, and then they aren't in the shadow.

Henry Abramovitch: Luigi Zoja writes, "Deep therapeutic healing is an ethical act, and every ethical act is indirectly therapeutic."

Murray Stein: That's very nice. I like that link between ethics and good therapy.

Henry Abramovitch: Rabbi Nachman writes: "If a man does not judge himself, all things judge him. They all become as messengers of God."

Murray Stein: The Rabbi's advice is to take those messengers of God on board seriously, to reflect on them. We get messengers about our shadow from many sides.

Henry Abramovitch: Jung felt that evil is very contextual. An overbearing mother who is controlling and doing everything for a son out of love and tenderness for this child, but for the child, this is clearly evil. In one sense, people who are Islamic terrorists, for instance, are in a group that feels they are doing a wonderful, holy, spiritual deed. I think it's important to remember what we feel is evil, someone may be seeing as an exceptionally good and sacred act. This very much also reflects the stage of a primal unity, I think as we have touched upon, which is you have harmed somebody in one group of nation, they therefore will harm anybody in your nation. And therefore, from their point of view, it makes moral sense to them, and that's why they're doing it. It happens almost every day in my part of the world where the goal is not to achieve peace but to hurt the other side.

Murray Stein: I think the solution lies in the realization that there are different perspectives and each has some merit and validity. If you fall into the splitting act of "we're good and they're bad," you fall back into Neumann's first stage of ethics. So much destructive behavior can be justified on that basis. A lot of that is fueled by fear, anger, and a need to have revenge. I think if we reflect on our own shadow projections and reactions and pull them back at least a bit, we can still defend ourselves. We can still seek justice and safety for people, but we don't do it with the same emotional energy and one-sided vindictiveness.

Henry Abramovitch: Maybe I'll be a little provocative. Most people in the West were very happy when bin Laden was killed. From a moral point of view, he should have been captured and put on trial. From the point of view of ethics, it was obvious.

Murray Stein: From an ethical point of view, yes, this is true. But it's very difficult. It's primitive justice, you know. You rejoice at the destruction of the evil enemy. Back to first stage, for sure!

Henry Abramovitch: Well, I think in some ways 9/11 was evil. That's not in question. Let me go back to the Bible and discuss scapegoat rituals. Priests put the sins of the people on the scapegoat, who was then led out to the Judean desert and thrown from a cliff. Another lesser-known, but more poignant, scapegoat ritual is described when one finds a murdered body lying in the field with no clue of the identity of the murderer. The elders of the closest town must sacrifice a bullock that has never been used for agriculture. Then, the elders lay their hands on the animal and declare, "Our hands are clean. We have no guilt in this matter." At first, it might seem like a straightforward scapegoat ritual, to purify the land from the evil that was done. But the Talmud does not take it at face value. They query: "What do you mean, they have on their hands no part in this bloodshed?" They continue questioning: "Does anybody actually believe they themselves murdered the man found in the field?" And the Talmud answers in a way to explore the responsible self. They ask: "Did we take responsibility for this stranger? When he left our town, did we give him food? Did we give him a guide? Did we tell him where the dangers were?" The view of the Talmud is not whether we engaged in bloodshed, but whether we do everything we could to protect him and prevent the tragedy from happening. In a sense. this connects with my workshops on ethics. We have to accept that violations can happen, but if we strengthen our ethical muscles by moral preparation, we will be more ready to deal with it when it does occur, to ourselves and to others. This is how the Talmud reads the ritual declaration, "Our hands are clean ..." It is not a statement of legal innocence but of ethical responsibility, namely: Did we do everything we could to protect him and prevent this atrocity? This assertive, ethical attitude links the responsible self to Neumann's New Ethic. And another argument from Neumann is that growth of consciousness will lead to increased moral understanding of an ethical area of which we have been unaware. Neumann famously was an early prophet of the ecological movement, seeing the Earth as our mother in need of protection. Genuine equality between woman and men was another topic that was dormant when Neumann wrote his book and since the Sixties has become urgent, although the roots may be found at the end of the Book of Job. Animal rights is another area of growing ethical awareness, and he felt that new areas of ethical sensitivity will necessarily develop as consciousness grows.

I want to end with a favorite quote by Jung: "One does not become enlightened by imagining figures of light, but by making the darkness conscious."[5]

---

[5] C.G. Jung, "The Philosophical Tree," CW 13, para. 335.

References

Dewald, P. A. & Clark, R. W. (2001). *Ethics Case Book of the American Psychoanalytic Association.* New York: American Psychoanalytic Association.

Jung, C.G. (1954/1967). "The Philosophical Tree." In *Collected Works*, vol. 13. Princeton, NJ: Princeton University Press.

Liebscher, M. (ed.). (2015). *Analytical Psychology in Exile. The Correspondence of C.G. Jung and Erich Neumann.* Princeton, NJ: Princeton University Press.

Kaplan, A.H. & Rothman, D. (1986). "The dying psychotherapist." *American Journal of Psychiatry.* 143(5): 561-572.

Neumann, E. (1969). *Depth Psychology and the New Ethic.* New York: G.P. Putnam's Sons.

Steinsaltz, A. (1977). *The Essential Talmud.* New York: Bantam Books.

Human Shadow Revealed by the Ecological Crisis

Brigitte Egger

Evil and shadow are mostly discussed regarding their painful implications for human beings. Accordingly, until recently they have mostly been an issue of spirituality, ethics, psychology, and law. But human evil and shadow impact nature just as cruelly. The present planetary ecological crisis bluntly reveals the unaddressed human shadow unconsciously acted out. We bitterly deplore the many current wars among peoples and nations, but we seem little aware of how much we are acting as if we were at war with nature.

Remarkably enough, today it is the sheer degradation of the environment, which is the very foundation of all life, that imperiously urges us to face the human shadow—past, present and future. Our era is marked by an exaltation of free human will without respect for a larger frame of reference, be it the transcendent, the biosphere, the Other inside or outside us—a respect that the crisis of the living planet is more and more dramatically calling for. The fundamental conclusion to draw is that the ecological crisis is also a spiritual crisis, an outer as well as an inner crisis, for the *outer* ecological crisis has its roots and solutions in the way we think and act, that is, in the *inner* human psyche. They are the two sides of the same uprootedness from the natural cycles, the same loss of awareness of the whole. They must therefore both be addressed together for the needed double turnaround.

I. Learning from Basic Life Patterns

Psyche and matter—inner nature and outer nature—mirror each other, disclosing their common root. Ecological patterns offer amazing amplifications to better understand psyche. They provide a kind of elemental ground to psychic functioning and thus healthy reference to clarify the nature of the human shadow and to better situate our problematic behavior. For consciousness allows us, if not seduces us, to transgress natural laws, even to the point of forgetting them. Yet in remarkable compensation, spiritual practices appear to put them at their core, namely in symbolic form. Before learning more about the human shadow from its pernicious effects on nature thanks to symbolic translation, let us get inspiration from some basic natural patterns as wholesome touchstones.

A. Active Relatedness and Complementarity

Life on Earth has created an amazing web or symphony of interconnectedness on a whole range of different levels, be it ecosystems, species, individuals, organs, or cells, each element acting in concert with the whole. This is already true for matter itself. Life evolved over millions of years to create this unique biosphere as we know it today, unfolding and differentiating into myriads of different and complex biological communities living in active relatedness and dynamic balance with their environment, soil, atmosphere, water, temperature, and sunlight, in ways essential for their survival. And as far as we can see, this living miracle might be the one and only. This basic interconnectedness can be regarded as a kind of primordial eros or love. No wonder that Dante not only describes all the dangers of human shadow and evil in terms of distorted love but concludes *The Divine Comedy* with his mystical experience of now being moved by the "love that moves the sun and the other stars."

This active relatedness is fruitfully captured in the creative principle of complementarity. Complementarity, as physicists put it, suggests that all mutually exclusive aspects are relevant to the whole, thus implying an underlying reality of unity. Further, everything that is manifest and concrete is fundamentally complementary, dual or plural, and limited, whereas unity, or wholeness, is transcendent. Once again, relatedness appears crucial, both between the complementary members and between the single element and unity. Humanly speaking, diversity requires courage and trust. Allowing the other to approach us as well as bearing our own otherness challenges us. It implies a great deal of conscious self-limitation and respect for the other, that is, of love. Indeed, the union of opposites spoken of so often by Jung on the psychological level is nothing less than a principle of life and evolution. It is therefore a dangerous illusion to force unity by excluding or ignoring the opposite. One-sidedness always produces something cast out, rejected, repressed. On the contrary, imagining all conceivable complements is deeply heuristic. True unity, be it inner or interpersonal, can only be achieved through a maximum effort to unite all opposites. Complementarity can thus be understood as a natural ethical principle.

B. Renewal through Death

Nature and life can be both sublimely beautiful and utterly ruthless. Indeed, the basic interplay between life and death, eating and being eaten, is the driving force that assures the renewal of life. Predator and prey, growth and decline, creativity and destruction, light and shadow, all follow the same creative interplay of opposites. Most of nature's creatures die in a brutal way. Eating signifies the death of a living being, plant or animal. We all therefore share in the violence of nature. This prompts the question of our contribution to the planet in exchange for the goods we draw from it—and more profoundly, the question of the task of humankind in the cosmos.

Similarly, birth and death of organisms succeed one another along the ancestral genealogical chains—from acorn to oak to acorn. This is the core principle on which the evolution of life rests, the very archetype of creative transformation. The advent of sexual reproduction, in other words the genial appearance of marriage with "another" of the opposite sex, intensifies change by introducing genetic intermingling. Each new individual starts anew from a so-called totipotent egg cell, i.e., from a concentrated undifferentiated quasizero, a kind of big bang in miniature. This resetting to zero, which allows successive adaptation to a constantly evolving environment, is a frequent pattern in biology, such as the principle of compost that reverts to fertilizer, or of the dead leaf of a tree replaced by a fresh gem. As passage through a symbolic death, it lies at the very heart of spiritual paths, from initiation to religious vows. One version is the famous "beginner's mind" in Zen Buddhism.

C. Nature's Laws Limiting Excesses or Transgressions

Living organisms, and matter even more strictly, respect the laws of nature, its cycles and interconnections, in a remarkably stable manner. A fine example are the organs, which work as in an orchestra for the benefit of the whole body. (Suggestively, the word organ referred originally to a musical instrument, later it informed the idea of organization.) In natural environments, animals do not behave in any excessive manner. Moreover, contrary to humans who wage war against their fellow beings, warm-blooded animals avoid killing congeners and know rituals to ascertain the stronger and accept submission and safe retreat, respecting dominance. All of nature's forms show themselves fundamentally to be at one with their essence and thus fulfill their vocation while remaining embedded in their surroundings. Their behavior can be called naturally ethical.

These rather regular cyclical ground aspects of life are accompanied by a slight but steady asymmetry toward evolution—and toward psychization with the emergence of consciousness and the rise of humans. Besides the regular intermingling in sexual reproduction, evolution progresses thanks to minute transgressions in the form of mutations in a single individual, that is, of rare alterations resulting from errors in the genetic information. Such a transgression is essential, for it is the only source of new genes and therefore of genetic diversity. Yet, any mutation is ruthlessly tested by natural selection and only kept if it offers a benefit for the whole. Nowadays, however, human creativity is frankly seduced by transgression with little regard for its repercussions on the planet. It seems important to remember that it is the individual that assumes a pivotal role for any transformation, be it biological or psychological, since change takes place within the single being who is the entity that lives it out.

II. Ethics and Wholeness, Evil and Excess

The basic biological patterns discussed above suggest simple definitions of evil and ethics, taking into account both the human and the natural realm. Defining ethics as a quality or behavior aiming at the creative benefit on the largest possible scale enables us to capture an evolutionary principle deeply rooted in the universe. It is the innate principle that makes organs work for the benefit of the whole body, or the natural constituents of hydrogen that allow a cascading creation of the other elements building up the cosmos. In this sense, ethics directly implies a relationship first to the other surrounding elements and therefore, implicitly, a relationship to wholeness—and thus embodies the creative principle of complementarity.

Evil, for its part, can be defined as the contrary of ethics: It takes no account of the interests of the other, or of the whole, and is out of balance, excessive. Meaningfully enough, the word evil itself has an etymological root with the meaning of going beyond, transgressing, being excessive. Since natural biological systems have been described as naturally ethical, and taken as reference, it makes sense to restrict the qualifying as evil strictly to the judgment of human behavior. As for the human shadow, it can be seen as the unlived life.

Like everything unconscious, it appears easily projected outside, accompanied by negative effects. The shadow can become a gateway to evil. But distinguishing shadow from evil is a delicate matter and beyond the scope of this article.

III. Dramatic Human-Induced Ecological Degradation

Let me now sketch a picture of the extent of the ecological degradation of the planet. For life on earth, the most worrying ecological issue is the human-induced biodiversity loss, often called the sixth mass extinction. It is even more worrying than climate change, which is only one of its causes. We humans are cornering nature through our exploitation of space and resources, through pollution and waste, and through sheer overpopulation. Let me evoke some cardinal aspects, remembering with Dante that transformation starts with passing through Hell with open eyes to better recognize what is contrary to life and has to be avoided.

In terms of land use, almost half of the world's nonbarren land is used for agriculture, that is, with a limited number of species of animals or plants: Livestock requires three-quarters of this land, whereas crops for human use only one quarter. By contrast, the remaining forests, the green lungs of the Earth, cover a much smaller area than agriculture, and primary or intact forests a vastly smaller area than crops alone.

In terms of their biomass, wild mammals left on Earth amount to a tiny 4 percent compared to 60 percent farmed mammals, and 36 percent humans. This constitutes a reduction by two-thirds in a century and 90 percent since before the megafaunal extinction on all the continents except

Africa following the rise of humans. Also, small creatures such as insects have suffered dramatic losses, with cascading consequences for food webs and "ecosystem services," such as providing pollination for plants to bear fruit or food for birds. Flying insects, again in terms of their biomass, have diminished by three-quarters over only the last three decades in Germany, and this in protected areas.

The overall conclusion is sobering: The ecosystems of the planet are unlikely to be able to support future generations.

IV. Ecological Price of Consciousness and Civilization

The hallmark of the human species is the birth of consciousness out of instincts, like a mirror revealing a second inner planet. Consciousness has allowed us to gain a growing freedom from the constraints of nature and a flourishing imagination and creativity, but it has come at the price of gradually losing our innate embeddedness in the natural cycles and of growing shadow effects. Correspondingly, the twin of consciousness has been religiosity, which aims at reconnecting us with the lost wholeness. Alongside the loss of worship of nature divinities and of the Great Goddess, we have increasingly exploited the environment, hardly considering the wider ecological consequences, and are now stumbling against them. We may wonder how deeply the drive to prevail over nature is ingrained in us. The oldest significant sign, which is the extinction of most of the large land mammals (e.g., mammoths), follows the rise of humans about 50,000 years ago, when our ancestors numbered fewer than a few million.[1] No other species is so hegemonic and manifests such a long shadow.

The evolution of the cosmos appears as one irresistible aspiration toward a higher degree of freedom, accompanied by an increase in complexity. This is particularly perceptible in the evolution of life, but it was already present at the dawn of the cosmos with the creation of atomic elements from hydrogen and then of molecules from atoms. Yet human freedom, boosted by the advent of consciousness, seems to be the first to cross a threshold where the relationship to the whole gets lost. Human behavior and productions cease to be integrated for the benefit of the whole and become increasingly destructive, threatening the very fabric of life.

Symbolically, as when working with dreams in analysis, we understand mastering our inner animals, our inner nature, as mastering our instincts or unconsciousness, and sacrificing the animal as sacrificing our unconsciousness in service of a higher purpose—inner and outer nature mirroring each other. Yet the present ecological situation shows how the drive to prevail over nature has been vastly more material than psychological or spiritual. Symptomatically, after learning to hunt like predators, humans turned to hunting other humans as warriors and to exploit the environment excessively. This challenges the idea of our ancestral harmony with nature. And how can we know what price nature herself is willing to pay? Humankind has been seduced into a state of hubris. Our consciousness and the ensuing civilizations have come at the heavy expense of the environment. And now we encounter the inescapable limits of nature, and she herself obliges us to turn the tide, to shoulder the responsibility for

---

[1] For ecological data overview see e.g., https://ourworldindata.org.

the demanding gift of consciousness and put ourselves at her service. A better balance between outer and inner, between material and soul dimensions, is desperately needed. To foster this balance, the new territory to discover and develop is the inner planet. The shadow must be faced. Why not dare imagine a future that is more mystical than technological?

V. Shadow, Excess, and Transgression in Myths: Examples

A. The Danger of Excess: Actaeon the Hunted Hunter

Hunting is a fundamental and eloquent symbol for the exploitation of nature. It is a yearning to gain power over another life that permeates all human culture, from warfare as man-hunting, to sport as symbolic hunting, to love and spirituality, which appeal to its attributes. The words for hunting and the goddess of love—venery and Venus—but also venerate, wish, win, all draw on the same etymological root encompassing the idea of striving after, wishing, desiring, being satisfied. Such ardent desire easily degenerates into excess, greed. Therefore, not surprisingly, hunting myths regularly thematize avidity. Most cultures living close to nature know laws and taboos concerning hunting, mirroring the respect for natural balance or nature's divinities.

Artemis, the Greco-Roman goddess who watches over nature and hunting, ferociously kills anyone who does not respect her, such as the frenetic hunter Actaeon.[2] While looking for a place to rest during one of his impetuous deer hunting parties, Actaeon enters the sacred territory of Artemis and surprises her bathing in the woods. Outraged by

---

[2] Ovid, *Metamorphoses,* III: 131-250.

this transgression, the goddess transforms him into a stag and condemns him to be devoured by his own maddened hounds, which no longer recognize him. On Greek vases, Actaeon is usually accompanied by Lyssa, the personification of frenzy, fury, and rabies.

The punishment of Actaeon for excess, avidity, and transgression teaches us that when we pursue a goal excessively and become unable to contain or limit ourselves, or respect the Other, we no longer control the situation and get possessed, in other words become destructively unconscious. It means entering a divine realm, a sanctuary, where the gods or nature dictate their laws. Here the dogs, as the driving instinctive forces that might be our helpful allies, turn against us and devour us. This motive of the hunted hunter offers a clear diagnosis: Avidity and arrogance are an illusion of power that ends up possessing and destroying us. As we have seen, evil is linked with the meaning of going beyond, transgressing. Artemis, who can be listened to as the voice of nature, demands the recognition of limits and inviolable zones.

What about our excessive invasion and eviction of natural habitats, which has furthered the recent pandemic? The unrestrained use of fossil energy and climate change, of nuclear energy and radioactive waste? The obsession with economic growth and the ensuing depletion of natural resources? Where does genetic engineering recognize sacred areas in life and nature? Let us listen to a later myth that works out a response.

B. Spiritual Turnaround: St. Hubert, Hunter Turned Religious

Hubert, like Actaeon, starts out as a passionate hunter. While hunting in the Ardennes Forest on Holy Friday, he sees that the beautiful white stag he is pursuing has a luminous crucifix between its antlers. Suddenly the deer stops and turns to face him. Hubert hears a strong voice urging him to renounce his unbridled passion and to pursue the salvation of his soul and not wild animals. And he converts. St. Hubert has become the patron saint of hunters and is venerated to this day in Europe—paradoxically, as a hunter who renounced literal hunting. Echoing his excessive past, he is also a protector against rabies and other aggressive diseases. "Hunting like St. Hubert" requires the hunter to observe self-limitation and to express respect for the game even in death.

As pre-Christian beliefs remained alive in the mountains and wild forests, certain features of St. Hubert's legend are reminiscent of the cult of Diana-Artemis as well as of the Wild Hunt of Wotan, the Germanic god whose name means fury or rage and who presides on the one hand over warlike fury and on the other over visionary and poetic ecstasy. As for the invulnerable stag, protector of inviolate nature, it is a basic European theme and is precisely the sacred animal of Artemis, who sometimes transforms herself into a stag. Seeing the crucifix on the stag can mean, on the one hand, realizing that nature is also impregnated with spirit and soul, is sensitive to suffering and hence fosters respect. On the other hand, it may stand for discerning the personal sacrifice to be made within ourselves, like Hubert who radically changes his life and turns his animal hunting pursuit into a spiritual pursuit. Like Artemis, the story of St. Hubert thematizes the mastery of wild impulses, yet explicitly states that the purpose is to turn them into a soul quest, coupled with compassion for all creatures.

Symbolically, tracking, killing, butchering, and eating an animal can be understood as becoming conscious of an instinctive drive. The next step is to extract the spiritual significance and meaning contained in it and then to draw practical consequences, taking into account the larger context. The final duty is to honor the sacrificed being or object by creating something out of it for the benefit of our surroundings. In this sense, the hunt in itself is a call to spiritualization and full of regard for the concrete dimension. The legend of St. Hubert therefore proposes not only to distinguish between the hunt for material goods and the spiritual hunt, but also to make a radical shift from the one to the other thanks to introspection, as shown by the stag's volte-face. The pivotal point of the turnaround and of awareness is once again the stag, that ancient guide to shamanic journeys with its marvelous antlers, which it sacrifices every year as long as it is fertile, and which thus symbolizes the vital renewal that ensures fertility.

In other words, this legend argues for material decrease in favor of spiritual growth. It urges us to place the exploitation of nature—and, likewise, the protection of the environment—in a spiritual and inner perspective. In short, St. Hubert and his divine sister Artemis are magnificent personifications of the principle of ecology and sustainable development, anchored in a spiritual dimension. To hunt in accordance with them is to limit oneself to a respectful exploitation of nature, while asking oneself if it helps the blossoming of the spirit, the soul, and the heart.

Does this legend not discreetly reveal to us the project meant for us here on Earth?

C. The Danger of Hubris: Arachne, Slave to Her Technique

Arachne is a masterful young weaver who boasts of her skills as an own achievement and not as a divine gift.[3] She even defies Athena, goddess of crafts, war, and wisdom, by surpassing her. Offended, Athena challenges Arachne to a weaving contest. Athena weaves a design showing the gods in all their power and glory, and adds in the corners the sad destiny of some pretentious mortals turned into animals. Arachne, on her side, pictures a lush universe of humans abused by the gods perfidiously shown as animals. Furious about the superior achievement of her mortal rival and about her displaying the flaws of the gods, Athena ransacks the tapestry and hits the girl with her shuttle. Arachne in despair hangs herself with the tattered threads of her work. Out of pity, Athena revives her, only to transform her into a spider, forever condemned to weave and to hang on the threads of her technique.

Consciousness allows us great freedom of creativity, yet it gets dangerous when we excessively defy or deride the creative divinity, the Great Web Master, and instead of a dialogue with it, we put ourselves above it. Then the threads of fate, the ineluctable natural laws, which we thought we were the masters of, end up ensnaring us. Fate leads who accepts it, drags who refuses it. It seems that no thought has been given to a possible shadow.

How could we fail to see the parallels with the creation of the Inter*net* and the World Wide *Web*, based on digitalization, this transition from the analogue to data expressed only in numbers. Feeding on a kind of hope of salvation through

---

3 This Greek myth is best known in the version of Ovid's *Metamorphoses,* VI: 1-145.

technology, the Internet in its early days promised to be a space of peaceful and creative exchange, bringing humans together, where collective and positive intelligences would flourish. No thought seems to have been given to a possible shadow. It looks as if the energy-transforming power of the living symbol is nowadays largely projected onto technology, just as the connection with the invisible and the beyond is projected onto the Internet and the mobile phone. Yet, the truth is that digital technology has made us dangerously dependent, transparent, and controllable. And the Internet is proving to be a vulnerable monopoly, which has opened the floodgates to sordid shadow and crime, and comes with a huge cost in energy, raw materials, waste, and financial resources. Digitalization affects all areas of life, replacing relationships to people and natural reality with autistic functionality and disembodied virtuality. Instead of technology serving human development, humans must increasingly adapt to technology. And here we are, as the myth of Arachne teaches us, bewitched into a humble spider, hanging on our creation, that is, a sad unconscious victim—a human bewitched into an animal—rather than a happy and responsible link in the fabric of the universe. Champions of rationality who relativized the relationship with the gods, the ancient Greeks have a particularly rich mythology of retribution for hubris.

D. Dealing with the Shadow of Technology: The Devil's Bridge

The famous Swiss St. Gotthard Pass traversing the Alps involves crossing a wild, steep-sided gorge. The Devil's Bridge there, erected in stone in 1595 to replace an unstable timber footbridge, was indeed a significant technical achievement. According to the legend,[4] the valley people, despairing about how to construct the bridge, called on the country council, which, not knowing better, wished out of spite to ask the Devil to do it. And there he came and offered to build it on the condition that the first soul to cross would be his. So, it happened, and the Devil waited for his reward. But a wise council member brought his stubborn male goat that impetuously leapt across the bridge. Furious at the trick, the Devil tears the goat to shreds and goes to fetch a gigantic stone to smash the bridge to pieces. A little grandmother, coming along, recognizes the fiend by his goat leg. She suggests he put down the heavy burden to catch his breath, and quickly she draws a cross on the stone. No matter how the Devil tears and pulls, the boulder will not budge. Howling with rage, the Devil sinks into the ground and disappears.

This legend illustrates beautifully how to avert technical progress from turning devilish, that is, life and soul-despising. In truth, each step of cultural or scientific progress, each gain in consciousness, threatens to cost a loss of soul and instinct if it is not balanced by an attentiveness to the larger ecological and spiritual context. More generally, raw creative energy is potentially dangerous and turns out truly constructive only if ethically directed.

In this tale, the authority, the reigning collective drive for such a daring project, carelessly appeals to the Devil, to an intelligence that may reveal itself to be the enemy of life and soul, turning us away from the divine. In this story, two people engage personally to banish the danger. First, the

---

[4] See T.Abt, *Progress Without Loss of Soul.*

down-to-earth goatherd takes the threat of losing a human soul to heart and is ready to make the conscious personal sacrifice of his shadow animal. His male goat may stand for the domestic little devil in our own shadow barn, aggressive and stubborn in the pursuit of his small selfish advantages or power, blinded and inflated by technological achievements or devices. Second, the humble old lady, wisely discerning evil, simply acts by using a religious symbol, disclosing a living relationship to the larger dimension. The sign of the cross, in the Christian faith a calling to God, is often used to ward off evil and symbolizes a conscious orientation actually based on suffered conjunction of opposites. The old lady may stand for nature and tradition that can agree with the creation of the bridge and contribute to consolidate it—which for us is a precious symbol of the passage of information from the unconscious to consciousness and vice versa. As for the Devil's fury, it may give us an idea of the aggressive potential of such technological genius, even prone to destroy its own creation.

Summed up, the lesson from this legend about a technological promise—think of plastic, or atomic energy—is, first, to sacrifice our personal power shadow, like the shortsighted benefit, or selfish gain, for our personal shadow is the entrance door to evil; and, second, to cultivate a religious attitude, an openness to the larger meaning of our presence on Earth—both central aspects of ethics. Thus, to turn out positive, technological development calls for an even more evolved soul development. Here we may recall the lesson from St. Hubert's legend.

VI. Psych-ecological Reading of Projected Shadow: Examples

Ecological problems unveil in telling images the human shadow of unlived soul life. Accordingly, a psychecological analysis of an issue does not provide an immediate program focused on a narrow ecological outcome. It rather situates it in a larger context. Although dissimilar in their outward implications, the following examples reveal a common inner core, and thus the possibility of addressing them synergistically at their root, along with many other ecological issues. No wonder, for nature is one interconnected whole, and ecological themes often amplify each other, perhaps even more visibly than cultural themes.

A. Light Pollution and the Neglected Mystery of Darkness

The changeable alternation between night and day marks the life rhythms of all organisms living on the surface of the Earth, in the sky, and in the upper reaches of marine waters. It is not limited to direct daily effects but extends to their seasonal rhythms through its influence on the internal clock of organisms. It is not confined to individual species but encompasses their interrelatedness and ultimately shapes entire ecosystems. Thus, depending on the duration of daylight, many plants grow or loose leaves, flower, build up reserves, or come to rest. Animals, too, experience their typical daily and seasonal rhythms of waking and resting, mating, feeding, and hunting.

Light pollution, which spreads out into the darkness of the night environment, disrupts these rhythms, alters relationships between species, and hinders behavior that has evolved over millions of years. For example, artificial light magnetically attracts insects at night and exposes them to increased predation; it also hinders the natural migration of birds that orient themselves by the stars. The starry sky of the Milky Way used to draw humans to contemplation. That light pollution blinds us now to the celestial lights is a sad caricature of our collective aberration: energy wasted in projection.

We associate light with consciousness and darkness with the unconscious, the unknown, and invisible. Fear of night, if not fear of death, is one of the drivers of excessive lighting and hinders its reduction to actual sober needs. In our civilization, the emphasis on rationality and control has eclipsed the principle of the night, the introverted, dark, and regenerative part of the life cycle, and has ended up breaking the vital relationship between the opposites that alternate and complete each other: between light and shadow, spirit and matter, and, above all, between good and evil.

Therefore, the symptoms of light pollution can be interpreted as a call to a twofold task. The first corresponds to the myth of the creation of light out of darkness in the psychological sense (not with lamps!): It is the quest of developing a personal conscience that avoids being blindly misled by collective behavior or immediate instinctive impulses but develops and affirms its own position, sheds light on its own shadow, and takes responsibility for it. The second task corresponds to the arduous, yet fundamental, myth of the night sea journey. It means acknowledging death and decrease, mystery and the unknowable, as integral parts of the life cycle. This active confrontation with the darkness necessary for regeneration relativizes the conscious ego and gives way to a deeper wisdom, expressed by the ethical attitude of service to a higher good that transcends the individual.

The movement pleading for the rehabilitation of the dark sky mirrors, perhaps unknowingly, the inner mystical longing.

B. Fear of the Wolf and Loss of Initiatory Reconnection with Our Roots

Humans have an emotionally charged and polarized relationship with wolves. It ranges from veneration and identification as a mythical ancestor to visceral hatred, now mainly in rural areas. In Europe, the wolf has been so severely persecuted that it has disappeared from most of the continent. Now protected, it is recovering and penetrating areas where shepherds are inexperienced with its predations. In Switzerland, for example, the wolf polarizes in an irrational manner. Wolves practically never attack humans. Yet they arouse greater fear than do cars. This shows emblematically how wolf and car are influenced by totally different unconscious representations, which can, however, be clarified by symbolic analysis.

Ecologically speaking, the wolf, like all great predators at the top of a food chain, plays an essential role in the equilibrium among species in nature. It controls herbivore populations and keeps them healthy and assures thereby a balanced development of vegetation. Culturally, animals are among the oldest divinities, for humans have perceived in them the wisdom and energy of the instincts that they lost through differentiating consciousness. Accordingly, the drama of predator and prey, of assertion and sacrifice, death and rebirth—or once again, day and night—appear as age-old themes of rituals and myths. Generally, the symbolic predator represents the fundamental instinctive and creative life urge, with its masculine side involving self-assertion, development of ego ,and consciousness, as well as its regenerative feminine side involving death and rebirth and initiatory reconnection with the instinctual roots. The highest form of human fulfillment is to unify these two sides on a higher plane. When the two sides are in balance, the predator represents the capacity to consciously abide by self-limitation and to sacrifice "ego will" in favor of a higher value. However, when the two sides are greatly unbalanced, the predator assumes the feature of the "all-devouring monster" with life energy discharging itself unconsciously as aggression and greed. This raises the ethical question of the right form to give to this creative energy—in other words, the question of good and evil.

Attaining a balanced "wolfishness" should help us to assert ourselves more spontaneously and convincingly, to concentrate on essentials and on being creative as well as personal, to radically free ourselves from the old and unnecessary, to be more sincere and more open to new situations, and to connect ourselves to the larger contexts.

Our deep-seated fear of the wolf in Europe has to do with the dark nature of the werewolf. In warlike cultures, fertility-stimulating ecstasy developed into battle-fury, and male initiation societies turned into warrior societies. Indo-Europeans equated the members of the latter with werewolves. With an increasingly one-sided patriarchization and an overemphasis on the outer material world, the fertility-stimulating wolf turned into the murderous werewolf, removed from its potential to serve as a spiritual antidote. The modern unrelenting fascination with the werewolf motif (as well as with crime stories) testifies to the challenge and vitality of the neglected corresponding psychic reality, which manifests itself also in violent crime, environmental pollution, greed, and exploitation, that is in a mania for conquest, control, and power.

The materially successful and extraverted West stresses the masculine and the ego, but it greatly undervalues the transcendent, the introverted, the very basis of life as well as self-limitation in favor of the whole. Inner values are therefore projected outward. We consistently overlook the devouring, wolfish shadow side of our culture such as, for example, our shameless irresponsibility, our insatiable craving for material goods, money, and recognition, our pretentious identification with "divine" attributes, and our lack of genuine care for the well-being of our planet and our souls. We face, as a result, very serious problems such as widespread psychic distress, ethical underdevelopment, and the destruction of the basis of life.

To be afraid of these developments appears to be a healthy reaction. However, it is illegitimate to project this dreaded one-sided inner wolf onto the outer animal. The sharp contrast between this shadow-wolf that is associated with unlimited and devouring greed, and the biological wolf that personifies the right balance, tells how strong, and therefore unconscious, this projection is. This is why the wolf problem is such a delicate and highly emotional subject: It touches the very moral foundations of our society.

Biological and psychomythical dimensions should be accorded equal treatment and their differences discussed. There is little point in using reason to try to fight inner images or psychic premises or in ridiculing them, since the psychic energy inherent in an image cannot be destroyed but only understood and transformed. Translating mythical representations into everyday situations, that is, psychologically, is quite effective. The greed and aggressiveness inspired by wolf images should be addressed and counterbalanced by mentioning the other pole of the symbolic wolf, which is courage and a willingness to make sacrifices.

So, the wolf as well as its return are actually bringing us a topical message: a call for self-limitation and reconnection with our roots.

C. Ecological Core Issues Carrying Projected Shadows of Unlived Life

Nowadays we have tragically lost the dimension of the soul and symbolic understanding. This means that key psychological values appear unconsciously projected at a concretistic level onto the core themes of economy, politics, science, technology, sports, and everything consumable to an astounding degree. We overcharge them with importance and mostly with destructive consequences. The symbolic analysis of different ecological and societal issues, taken as symptoms, unveils in speaking images the unlived soul life of our time, that is, the shadow of our time. Yet fortunately, it also helps to develop more deeply grounded perspectives. Here are some examples of psychic values and needs—and the concrete fields carrying their projections:

—-necessity of development and differentiation of consciousness—displaced on to excessive urbanization and diminishment of nature; on economic compulsion to (unlimited) growth, progress, on the controversial idea of underdevelopment;

—-necessity of mobilizing and mastering psychic energy—
displaced on to the obsessive search for sources and
control of material energy (e.g., money, petrol, water);
on atomic energy with its dangerous and long-lasting
waste;

—-symbolic life as means to transform psychic energy—
displaced on to the pull and tyranny of technology as
means to take hold of material energy and control its
transformation; search for wholeness and unity;

—-on money as a unique reference—displaced on to
globalization of the market; on Internet monoculture;
on agri-monoculture;

—-idea of creation of life—displaced on to genetic
engineering and its aberrations; on energy-consuming
"artificial intelligence";

—-idea of eternity—displaced on to chemistry and eternal,
nondegradable, often toxic substances (plastic etc.).

Analytical psychology offers invaluable tools and
deep insights into the unconscious and for bringing to
consciousness inner representations, for recognizing and
taking back destructive projections thanks to symbolic
understanding. These are precious resources for the
doubly needed and closely linked ecological and personal
turnaround.

VII. Reconnecting with the Dimension That Transcends Us

A. Turnaround and Consciousness Required by Nature

It is impressive to see how the acceleration of the
destruction and trivialization of nature has gone hand
in hand with a fading relationship to the divine and the

feminine principle of relatedness in favor of a materialistic scientific worldview and of rationality. The accompanying technological and medical developments have given increasing importance to the human individual and to human consciousness, promoting a dissociation from our natural roots and a growing utilitarianism that degrades nature to mere resources at our disposal.

But the impact of human activities has started to boomerang. The very culture that dreams of growth without limits, or freedom without reference to something transcendent, is now summoned not so much by an inner, personal religious call as by the very outer ecological crisis: It must revise its premises and learn to respect the larger dimension of given natural boundaries and cycles. Climate change and COVID-19 appear to be the first personally felt global irruption of the consequences of our disrespect for nature. It is a clear call for a comprehensive turnaround.

We are increasingly obliged to consciously manage the environment and actively perform functions that nature previously spontaneously provided: from introducing oxygen into polluted lakes to breeding and reintroducing decimated animals. We will increasingly become dependent on highly demanding scientific knowledge unless we work at healing from the roots—toward radical material simplification.

B. Ecological Sufficiency Mirrors Spiritual Practices

Remarkably, the ecological sufficiency needed as response to the outer crisis is mirrored in many features of traditional spiritual practices and even religious vows. Both ecology and spirituality—just like analysis—aim at reconnecting us with lost wholeness, therefore, with relativizing ego and consciousness. I hope that eco-sufficiency will soon also explicitly state that it is in favor of inner growth.

The double spiral, which might be the oldest symbol for the inner journey, expresses wonderfully the volte-face of self-reflection. The movement starts with an expansion from a center, sharply changes course, and winds back focusing on its core, rich with all the experience of the journey. For the first time, introspection becomes a necessity for collective material reasons. The confinement imposed during the pandemic can also be read in this perspective.

C. Recognizing the Divine in Nature and Matter

To safeguard life on Earth, we need to recognize that nature and matter are sacred and divine in their essence and enter in true and loving relationship with them. We are intrinsically part of nature: In us live old stardust and ocean brine and the traces of the whole genealogy of creatures and peoples from whom we are this unique offspring. What we eat matters inside and outside. Therefore, it seems that not only does the spirit want to be incarnated in us, but, as D. Baumann beautifully suggests, nature, or matter as well, wants to be made conscious through us, realized, loved, and fostered. The conscious choice to breed endangered species shows this sentiment so poignantly. This echoes Jung's encouragement to work toward a self-realization of the unconscious in our lives. It means asking what kind of self-realization nature wants. It means putting center stage the question of humanity's task and meaning in the universe.

*

To consider the ecological crisis as revealing the human shadow, that is, as symbolically expressing the unlived soul life, may offer a constructive perspective. It seems urgent to popularize the knowledge of the basic structures and dynamisms of the psyche—like projection and symbolic representation, complementarity and relatedness all linked—in order to systematically consider the other dimensions. This perspective is a largely untapped resource for the doubly needed ecological and psychological turnaround.

References

Abt, T. (2013). *Progress Without Losss of Soul. Toward a Holistic Approach to Modernization Planning*. Asheville, NC: Chiron Publications.

Baumann, D. (1997). "L'uomo parte conscia e quindi responsabile della nature?" In C. Widmann (ed.), *Ecologicamente*, Ravenna, Italy: Longo.

Egger, B. (2001). "Raubtiere, mythologisch und tiefenpsychologisch betrachtet." In *Humans and Predators in Europe* 76, 1/2: 53-90. Zürich: Forest, Snow and Landscape Research,

——. (2003). "Reading Collective Events: Ecological Issue of Energy and Globalization of the Market." In *Proceedings 15th International Congress for Analytical Psychology. Cambridge 2001*. Einsiedeln: Daimon Verlag.

——. (2006). "Radici e ramificazioni della caccia." *www. pronatura-ti.ch Rivista 9* (pp.1, 3-5, 16).

——. (2011). "Per un etica radicata nella natura." *www. pronatura-ti.ch Rivista 30* (pp.10 - 11).

——. (2017). "1. Il cervo, mitica guida. 2. Cervo: emblema della svolta ecologica." *www.pronatura-ti.ch Rivista 35* (pp.8-12, 16).

Ovid. (1955). *Metamorphoses*. London: Penguin Books.

About the Authors

HENRY ABRAMOVITCH, Ph.D. is Founding President and senior training analyst at the Israel Institute of Jungian Psychology in Honor of Erich Neumann, Professor Emeritus at Tel Aviv University and Past President of Israel Anthropological Association. He teaches Routers in the IAAP Developing Groups in Eastern Europe and Kazakhstan. He is author of *The First Father* (2010); *Brothers and Sisters: Myth and Reality* (2014); *Why Odysseus Came Home as a Stranger*... (2020) and forthcoming novella, *Panic Attacks in Pistachio*. With Murray Stein, he has written a number of plays including, *The Analyst and the Rabbi* and *My Lunch with Thomas,* available on Youtube. Since the beginning of the war, he has led a Reflection Group for Ukrainian Analysts on Zoom.

VALERIE APPLEBY is a Training Candidate at ISAP-ZURICH. Outside of this training program, her career has been spent in the publishing industry, with appointments at major publishers based in Toronto, New York, London and Cambridge (UK). Currently, she works as a Senior Commissioning Editor at Cambridge University Press, specializing in books for the social sciences. Her interest in Jung blossomed during her studies at the University of Toronto, where she focused on psychology, comparative religion and classical literature/mythology. These disciplines initiated her into a lifelong enquiry into the hidden and "unspeakable" aspects of our personal and collective experiences of the world. She is a dual US/UK citizen and maintains a permanent residence in the UK.

BRIGITTE EGGER, Ph.D. brings together ecology and Jungian psychology. Convinced since the Seventies that the environmental crisis is at its root a psychological problem, she searched inspiration from mystical literature to philosophy of science and discovered Jung and von Franz. Her research concentrates on the symbolic dimensions of ecological and collective issues, with special interest in the biological parents of psychic dynamisms. She works at introducing this healing perspective into practical environment protection, thus building up the field of psychology. She holds a doctorate in ecology and is a Jungian training and supervising analyst at ISAP-ZURICH, with a practice in Zürich. She is further interested in creativity at large and in creative ways to communicate depth psychological insights. And loves Dante.

MURRAY STEIN, Ph.D. was born in Canada and educated in the United States at Yale University and the University of Chicago. He is a graduate of the C.G. Jung Institute of Zurich and is presently a Training and Supervising Analyst at the International School of Analytical Psychology Zurich (ISAP-ZURICH). He has been president of the International Association for Analytical Psychology (2001-2004) and President of ISAP-ZURICH (2008-2012). He is the author of *Jung's Map of the Soul, Outside Inside and All Around, The Mystery of Transformation, Men Under Construction* and many other books and articles. He lives in Switzerland and has a private practice in Zurich and from his home in Goldiwil.

MARY TOMLINSON, J.D. graduated from ISAP-ZURICH in the spring of 2011 and commenced her private practice as Jungian psychoanalyst in her home city of Toronto, Canada in the same year. She served as President of the Ontario Association of Jungian Analysts from 2015 to 2018. Presently she is the Chair of the Ethics Committee of the Association of Graduates in Analytical Psychology. In 2023 she moved to Vancouver, British Columbia to join her children and is continuing her practice there. Her special interest is detective stories, about which she wrote her thesis at ISAP.

LUIGI ZOJA, Ph.D. received the Diploma from the C.G. Jung Institut Zürich (1974) and is a past President of the IAAP (1998-2001). He had a clinical practice in Zurich (1975-79), then a private practice in Milan and New York (2000-02) and presently in Milan. He has lectured internationally and has served as Visiting Professor at Beijing Normal University. He is the author of papers and books published in 15 languages. In English: *Drugs, Addiction and Initiation*, *Growth and Guilt*, *The Father* (Gradiva Award 2001),; *Cultivating the Soul*, *Ethics and Analysis* (Gradiva Award 2008), *Violence in History, Culture and the Psyche*, and *Paranoia. The Madness that Makes History*. The list of his books in Italian and Spanish can be found in Wikipedia.

www.ingramcontent.com/pod-product-compliance
Lightning Source LLC
Chambersburg PA
CBHW020705270326
41928CB00005B/276